30 GREAT RUNS IN LONDON

WELCOME TO 30 GREAT RUNS IN LONDON

GETTING STARTED

We think that London is one of the best cities in the world to run. The variety of scenery, depth of history, ease of access and sheers size of the place make it an infinitely varied running partner.

Yet this variety can make the choice of where to run bewildering. And we know how easy it is to get stuck in a rut running the same route over and over.

So, we've been all over Zones 1 - 3 to find 30 Great Runs that will help keep your training varied and your motivation high. Our criteria for including a route in the book were:

1. a variety of scenery to make it an interesting run
2. as much green space as possible
3. ease of access by public transport

That's what we think makes a great run. Easy to get to, picturesque and away from the traffic. Ultimately these are all runs we've either enjoyed regularly or loved discovering during researching and writing this book.

So we've got all the 'classic' running spots, from circling Richmond Park to looping along the Thames in Central London. But some of the real gems are off the beaten track through Victorian cemeteries, around less well-known country parks and along working waterways.

Whatever your reasons for choosing to go running, new routes will help keep your training fresh. Use this book, find new places. Explore, but most of all, enjoy your running.

PICKING A RUN

We've organised the book into five sections - north, south, west, east and central - each with six routes. So you can try different routes from across the city. The contents map (page 4-5) will help you see where the routes are.

For a bit of inspiration, try our Alternative Listings in the back of the book to find specific distances, hill climbs, river routes and great views.

Or, you can simply browse through and pick one that takes your fancy. Each run has an introductory page that highlights the route and summarises key information to help you chose the right one for you.

KEY FACTS

On the first page of each route there's a Key Facts box. This covers things like distance, hills, navigation, underfoot conditions, toilets, refreshments and transport links. An explanation of each of the Key Facts is on the inside front cover, but two are worth explaining in more detail.

✧ The navigation on the routes ranges from 'Easy' to 'Very difficult'. On the very difficult ones there might be only a few useful signs, or at certain points you'll have to set off in a particular direction without being able to see exactly where you're heading. The tougher the navigation, the more you'll need to pay attention to the route directions.

👥 We've classified some routes as places with 'Lots of people', others as 'Quite busy', 'Pretty quiet' and 'Very quiet'. We've used this to reflect how safe you might feel on the route - if there's lots of people it usually feels safer than if you're on your own. As a general rule, we'd recommend you do quieter routes with a friend first to get an idea of what they're like before venturing out solo.

ROUTE NAVIGATION

Each run features a double-page spread with the map and route all in one. Produced from Ordnance Survey and Collins maps with just the key details selected, the maps make it easy to get your bearings quickly.

Thumbnail photos pick out key points en route so you can see where to head and check you're on the right track. The directions are brief and to the point, so you don't have to spend ages wading through pages of information.

There's a key for the maps on the inside back cover for quick reference.

ADDITIONAL INFORMATION

Each route has additional information on transport, facilities and the local area.

Getting there - public transport to and from each run. We recommend you use the Transport For London Journey Planner website (www.tfl.gov.uk) to plan your route.

Opening times - some parks and public spaces have restricted opening time. These details are included so you can plan when to run.

Useful links and other info - extra information and websites that will help you get the most out of the run. Some of them are vital - for example, we'd recommend you check the British Waterways website for temporary closures if you're heading for a canal - others give you background details on selected sights along the route.

Signs and maps - some runs go through places where there are maps and info boards en route, others follow routes like the Capital Ring. We've pointed out where these help you navigate around the run.

Hills and climbs - so you can see how much up and down there is on each route (make sure you check the scale on each graph - they vary).

Refreshments, Toilets, Car and Bike Parking - where to find these if they're available.

CONTENTS

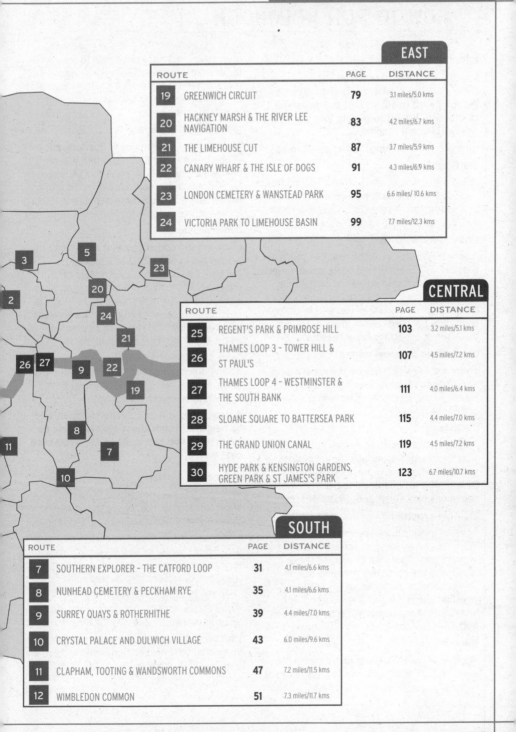

HOW TO RUN IN LONDON

Running safety

London is a great place to run but it's also a busy urban environment with risks attached. We don't want to put you off, but please be careful and take responsibility for your own safety whilst out running.

Here are some of things to watch out for.

Traffic and roads

There are no totally traffic free routes in this book so take care running alongside roads. Use pedestrian or zebra crossings wherever possible for crossing roads.

Underfoot conditions

Interesting routes avoiding roads as much as possible (like those in this book) cover varied terrain from cobbled streets to grass trails and uneven footpaths. Normal running shoes should be fine for most routes and most conditions but take care with your footing throughout, especially in bad weather.

Low bridges on canal routes

There are a few of these on the canal routes - you'll need to watch your head. Watch out for curved bridges where the height varies across the towpath.

Cyclists

Another hazard on towpaths and other waterside routes especially. Some cyclists don't use a bell, many don't slow down. Beware of bikes approaching from behind and run to one side of the path where possible.

Weather conditions

Some of these routes become impassable after very heavy rain, others become more slippery underfoot. We've marked those where this is a particular problem, but all routes become more dangerous in bad weather. Canal towpaths and parts of the Thames Path, particularly the rural sections in the west, become flooded after heavy rain.

Darkness

The most sensible thing is to not run in the dark. But we're not going to say 'don't run at night' because that's not useful advice - few of us have the luxury to be able to always run during daylight hours. But bear in mind that every other risk is significantly increased at night and you need to take extra care when out after dark.

Ipods and MP3 players

The equivalent of running in the dark, but for your ears. All risks increase when you can't hear what's going on around you. Again, we're not going to say 'don't listen to music' but be aware that it's more dangerous if you do and at least keep it turned down.

Other people

If you live in London you'll be aware that people have been attacked whilst out running. Although this is extremely rare, especially compared to the number of miles clocked up safely, you should do as much as possible to reduce the risk. Try to vary your route and when you run, take a personal alarm and if possible, don't run alone.

Aside from these risks, make sure you warm up and down properly, and if you're starting to run for the first time it's recommended that you talk to your doctor first.

Bottom line: you go running to get fit and be healthy - think about the risks and do everything you can to make sure you stay that way.

And finally...

We've checked all the runs in the three months prior to going to press in October 2006.

But things change rapidly in London. We've found closed Tube stations, reopened towpaths, new footpaths, moved signposts, renamed pubs and repainted buildings.

If you find directions that don't work, please let us know (enquiries@30greatruns.co.uk).

We'll happily check your amendment and if we include it in the next edition we'll send you a free copy as a thank you.

A tough but rewarding 5.5 mile run through playing fields, along reservoir paths and a great London country park

FRYENT COUNTRY PARK & WELSH HARP RESERVOIR

Rural landscapes for a change of pace

We think this is one of the locations that should be pretty high up your list of places to run. Yes, there are other bits of roughish ruralness around (Richmond Park springs to mind), but we think Fryent is the most wilderness-like space we've got inside Zone 3.

So what's it got? Proper countryside, with real old fashioned little fields and traditional hedgerows for starters. And then some decent woodland and a couple of good summits to climb.

Elsewhere this route heads along the path around Brent Reservoir, also known as Welsh Harp (after an 18th century pub that used to be around here). It's a popular and pleasant spot for a bit of sailing and you'll often see a few boats out on the water.

It is one of the harder routes to navigate around and there's some road running in between the green spaces. But if you fancy something genuinely different then head up to Hendon and try a loop of Fryent Country Park. Our guess is you'll want to go again.

KEY FACTS

🏃	5.3 miles / 8.5 kms
⇄	Loop
🍃	Playing fields, country park, reservoir path and roads
START FINISH	Hendon overland station
⏱	Unrestricted
⟷	Very difficult. Several tricky sections/open spaces with few signs
👟	Mixed – roughly half hard pavements half grass/trails
🏃🏃	Very quiet
⛰	Hilly – one significant climb
🚗	Several road sections, including main road running and busy road crossings
🚻	Off route
P	Near station
🚲	At station
🍴	En route

THE ROUTE

From Hendon station it's a short road section down to West Hendon Playing Fields, across Silver Jubilee Park and through Church Lane Recreation Ground. Back on the road again, you head up into Fryent Country Park, climbing up Gotsfords Hill for views across the park and beyond. It's then on for a steep climb up to the top of Barn Hill for a view of the new Wembley Stadium. A short road section leads you down to Welsh Harp Reservoir. After a quick tour, it's then back to the station to complete the route.

FRYENT COUNTRY PARK & WELSH HARP

5
A. At the end of Elthorne Way enter Church Lane Recreation Ground past a wooden gate
B. Follow the tarmac path right and circle around the park, then exit just before the children's playground (opposite where you came in)
C. Head up to the road and cross over into Slough Lane opposite (use the crossing on your right)

A. Continue on through a gap in the hedge (above)
B. Turn right and make your way diagonally across the park to a children's playground 250 metres away
C. Cross the road and head into Elthorne Way directly opposite the playground

6
A. Continue to the end of Slough Lane, then cross straight over and up the track (above) into Fryent Country Park
B. Head straight uphill beside the horse enclosure, then continue on following sign for 'Barn Hill'
C. Take the first gap in the hedge on the right up to the Capital Ring signpost on top of Gotsford Hill
D. From here follow the Capital Ring sign for 'Preston Park 2m'. Keep to the Capital Ring way markers all the way down to the main road

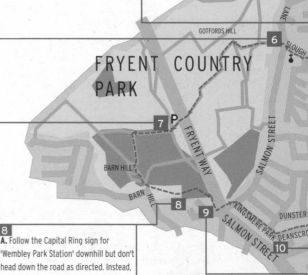

SLOUGH LANE

GOTFORDS HILL

6

SLOUGH

FRYENT COUNTRY PARK

7 P

FRYENT WAY

SALMON STREET

BARN HILL

BARN HILL

8

9

KINGSMERE PARK

DUNSTER D

DEANSCRO

SALMON STREET

10

7

A. Cross the road into the car park and follow Capital Ring signs up left past the Fryent Country Park information board, then right following a sign for 'Barn Hill'
B. Follow the Capital Ring sign straight on, then steeply uphill to the left to arrive at Barn Hill Pond (above)
C. Head around the pond to the signpost on the far side

8
A. Follow the Capital Ring sign for 'Wembley Park Station' downhill but don't head down the road as directed. Instead, continue dead straight on across the field in front of you to the far corner
B. At the corner, take the trail left into the woods (not the path on right with five wooden posts at it's top)
C. Continue on ignoring the first cross-path. The path bears left to a T-junction – turn right, then immediately left to get to the main road (Fryent Way)

9

A. Turn right and head down the main road to the roundabout. Cross over to the left, then take first left into the gated Salmon Street (above)
B. Take the first right down Kingsmere Park

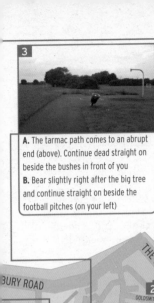

3

A. The tarmac path comes to an abrupt end (above). Continue dead straight on beside the bushes in front of you
B. Bear slightly right after the big tree and continue straight on beside the football pitches (on your left)

2

A. At the bottom of Goldsmith Avenue, enter the playing fields (signposted 'Hendon Film studios, cafe, bowls club')
B. Follow the main tarmac drive left then right, then along a tree-lined path (above). Bear right to the end of the path

1

A. At the top of the station access road turn right over the rail bridge
B. Take the first right down Wilberforce Road – church (above) on corner. Head straight on to the end. Turn left down Garrick Road
C. At the junction (Toyota garage on corner) turn right and head along past Halfords and Comet (on left)
D. Take the pedestrian crossing in front of Sainsbury's and then continue along to take the first left into Goldsmith Avenue

THE HYDE

BURY ROAD

SAINSBURY'S

START
FINISH

GOLDSMITH AVENUE

2

HALFORDS
COMET

Hendon

1

GARRICK ROAD

RUSSELL ROAD

WILBERFORCE RD

STATION ROAD

CHURCH NE REC ROUND
ND RNE ROAD

5

WAY
ELTHORNE
ALLOT MENTS

PLAY GROUND

3

4

PERRYFIELD WAY

TOWNSEND LANE

SILVER JUBILEE PARK

WEST HENDON PLAYING FIELDS

THE BROADWAY

The Harp

COOL OAK LANE

12

12

A. The path arrives at Cool Oak Lane (above). Turn right over the bridge (use pedestrian signals) and along the road
B. Continue up to the main road (Harp pub on right at the junction), then turn left along the main road
C. Continue on the left hand side. Head across Perryfield Way, then take the pedestrian crossing over the main road
D. Head straight into Station Road and follow it uphill back to Hendon station

WELSH HARP RESERVOIR

GARDEN CENTRE

P **11**

11

A. Head past the car park and take the main path right towards the reservoir (above)
B. Follow the path all the way along beside the reservoir on your right. Ignore paths to the left

CHEN GROVE
LANE

10

A. At the end of Kingsmere Park turn left (Deanscroft Avenue), then right at the main road (towards church spire)
B. Cross over in front of the church, then turn left into Old Church Lane.
C. Turn left again where the road bears right (still in Old Church Lane)
D. Head to the end (past the fence in road), then turn left (towards garden centre), then right past a green metal road barrier

FRYENT COUNTRY PARK & WELSH HARP

Getting there

The route starts at Hendon overland station.

Hendon is on the line to Luton and St Albans. The main connections in town are at King's Cross and Farringdon but trains also go through Blackfriars and London Bridge.

Check your route at the Transport For London website (www.tfl.gov.uk).

Hendon is in both Zones 3 and 4.

Opening Times

Access to this route isn't restricted by any specific opening times.

Useful links and other info

There is relatively little information about Fryent Country Park on the web. Barn Hill Conservation Group, who are very active in managing the Fryent landscape, have a website (www.bhcg.ik.com).

The route follows part of section 10 of the Capital Ring through Fryent Country Park. The Ring is one of the Greater London Authority's Strategic Walking Routes. You can use the TFL website to get more details and order leaflets (www.tfl.gov.uk/streets/walking/home.shtml).

Signs and maps

Aside from the Capital Ring signs, there are also others around Fryent - we've referred to them in the text where necessary.

Refreshments

There isn't much at the station. If you need to stock up, then we'd recommend popping into Sainsbury's on your way past, or there are shops in Hendon Broadway at the end of the run.

Toilets

There aren't any toilets at the station. Sainsbury's has toilets if you are shopping there.

Parking

The car park at the station is for permit holders only. There is metered parking in the roads near the station (typically £3 for 3 hours, Monday to Saturday, free at weekends).

Bike parking

There are cycle racks at the station.

Hills and climbs

Total ascent/ descent 95 metres

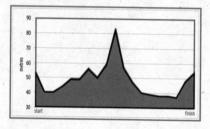

A 5.8 mile straight line cruise along the Regent's Canal with a little tour through Angel in the middle

REGENT'S CANAL FROM CAMDEN TOWN

London canal running at its best

The working waterways dotted through the city provide some fantastic, flat running well away from the hustle and bustle of the city. They've been mightily improved over recent years and are increasingly well looked after. You pass a number of permanently moored housesboats on this route and the London Canal Museum at Battlebridge Basin.

The Regent's Canal was built to connect up the Grand Union Canal's Paddington Basin in the west and the Thames in the east. Our route picks it up at Camden Town and follows the waterway from north London out east to Mile End.

In the middle of the route is the Islington Tunnel. It's three quarters of a mile length took six years to build. There's no towpath, so when the canal was built in the 1800s, boatmen would have 'legged it' through the tunnel (lying on their backs and pushing with their feet on the walls) whilst the horses went over the top. Although this is an interesting duathlon opportunity, we don't recommend swimming and so follow the horse route through the streets of Angel to pick up the canal again at the other side for the rest of the journey down to Mile End.

KEY FACTS

	5.9 miles / 9.4 kms
	Straight line
	Canal towpath and city streets
START FINISH	Camden Town Tube station Mile End Tube station
	Unrestricted
	Fairly easy. The start and finish are fine – the section through Angel slightly tricky
	All hard surfaces TOWPATHS SLIPPERY AFTER RAIN LOW BRIDGE HAZARDS
	Pretty quiet along the canal/ Lots of people through the street sections
	Undulating (more down than up)
	One road section in the middle, plus to and from the Tube at either end
	At start
P	None
	At station
	Near stations

THE ROUTE

From Camden Town tube station it's a short road stretch up to the canal. You're then following the canal for a decent section through to Islington Tunnel, where the route leads up and through the streets of Angel. You then rejoin the canal at the end of the tunnel and continue heading east. Continuing alongside Victoria Park and then Mile End Park, you then head up from the canal again to find the Tube station at Mile End.

REGENT'S CANAL FROM CAMDEN TOWN

A. Continue along Kentish Town Road (past Sainsbury's on right) and up onto the bridge with the canal below (above)
B. Cross the bridge, then drop down left onto the towpath
C. Head under the bridge you just crossed to begin the first stretch of canal running

A. Continue along for approx. 1.6 miles (St Pancras Lock is just over half way along)
B. The towpath ends at Islington Tunnel. Head left up the ramp and steps to the road (above)

MIDDLE – AROUND ANGEL

A. Exit Camden Town tube station by the Kentish Town Road exit - the Camden Eye pub (above) is opposite
B. Turn left along Kentish Town Road (signposted for 'MTV Centre')

A. Bear right across the road and head through a gate (above) along a footpath (basketball court on left, houses on right)
B. Continue up the path through housing estate and then head past the school (on left) to the end of Maygood Street
C. Turn right along Barnesbury Street

Navigation on this route

The bit around Angel in the middle is slightly tricky, so we've enlarged the map covering that section to make it easier to follow.

6

A. Turn right in front of The Mall Antiques Arcade (above) down Duncan Street
B. Head to the end of Duncan Street. Take the zebra crossing on left and go through the gate back down to the canal. Continue along the towpath

8

A. At the top of the steps head past the pub up to the main road. Turn left to pass under the Green Bridge (above)
B. At the main cross roads head straight over and then right using the crossings. Mile End station is 100 metres on the right

KINGSLAND BASIN

REGENT'S CANAL   REGENT'S CANAL

WENLOCK BASIN
TV ROAD
BASIN

VICTORIA PARK

OLD FORD ROAD

ROMAN ROAD

REGENT'S CANAL

MILE END PARK

New Bridge

8 Mile End

7

MILE END BRIDGE

GROVE ROAD

BURDETT ROAD

FINISH

7

A. Continue along the canal. This section is approx. 3.6 miles with Acton's Lock roughly half way along. Towards the end pass alongside Victoria Park, Old Ford Lock and Mile End Park
B. Immediately after Mile End Lock, take the steps up to the left (above) away from the canal

5

A. Continue along road, then take first zebra crossing over towards the Salmon & Compass pub (above). Head past pub into Chapel Market
B. At the end of Chapel Market turn right up to the road junction
C. Take the crossing over towards Angel Tube station but turn left away from the station along Upper Street

REGENT'S CANAL FROM CAMDEN TOWN

Getting there

The route starts at Camden Town Tube station, which is in Zone 2 on the Northern Line.

The end of the route is at Mile End Tube station, in Zone 3 on the Central Line.

If you need to get back to the start then it's about 25 minutes. Take the Central Line back into town and change onto the Northern Line at Bank.

Opening Times

The route doesn't pass through any areas affected by specific opening times.

Useful links and other info

Regent's Canal is looked after by British Waterways. There are occasional closures on the towpath, some of which are quite lengthy, so check their website before you set out (www.waterscape.com/boating/stoppages/).

London's Canal Museum is well worth a visit and their website has an interesting history of the Regent's Canal and the Islington Tunnel (www.canalmuseum.org.uk).

Signs and maps

The canal is fairly well signposted, with most bridges and locks named. Things like nearby stations are pointed out along the way.

The Islington Tunnel road section is waymarked on the pavement with a round sign showing the way. We find these a little confusing, so we'd recommend following our route rather than the underfoot symbols.

Refreshments

There are shops at both the start and finish of the route.

Toilets

There are toilets near Camden Town Tube station, in the pedestrian islands at the junction with Camden High Street. Follow the signs from the station.

Parking

Parking is generally tricky around Camden and so we don't recommend driving to this route.

Bike parking

There is cycle parking outside Camden Town Tube station.

Hills and climbs

Total ascent 23 metres
Total descent 38 metres

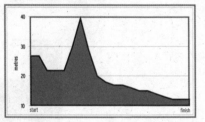

A simply fantastic 5.5 mile straight line run incorporating former rail lines, ancient woodlands and the popular Alexandra Palace

FINSBURY PARK TO ALLY PALLY

The north at its heights

This is one of the highlights of the North section. The Parkland Walk - a thin strip of green curving between Finsbury and Alexandra Parks - makes it a virtually all-green route that's surprisingly quiet given the bustle of the surrounding area.

Formerly the Northern Heights Railway, there were plans to incorporate the line into the Tube network. But it closed in the 1970s, reopening in 1984 as a nature reserve. It now creates a leafy link between the two parks, especially when you add in the ancient forests of Queen's and Highgate Wood half way along.

At the top you can't miss Alexandra Palace. Regarded fondly by locals and gig-goers alike, it opened in 1863 as north London's version of the Crystal Palace, housing art galleries, lecture theatres and a concert hall. Like the Crystal Palace, it was destroyed by fire - but this one was rebuilt and has gone on to be a popular entertainment venue.

On a clear day you can see right across London from Alexandra Palace. The TV masts of Crystal Palace, visible on the horizon some 13 miles away, provide a further link between the two grand old Palaces.

KEY FACTS

	5.6 miles / 9.0 kms
	Straight line
	Parks, woods, fantastic buildings, a few roads and lots of converted railway
START FINISH	Finsbury Park Tube/overland station Alexandra Palace overland station
	Restricted
	Quite tricky. The sections through Queen's Wood and Highgate Wood are criss-crossed by lots of trails
	Mixed – solid paths or grass options in the parks, elsewhere tarmac pavements and trails
	Pretty quiet throughout
	Very hilly – pretty much up hill all the way
	Some traffic and road crossings
	At start and near route
P	Nearby
	Opposite station
	Near start and en route

THE ROUTE

From the station you're almost immediately into Finsbury Park itself for a short section up to join the Parkland Walk, following the Capital Ring for a few miles. Further on, leave the rail line for a short road section past Highgate Tube station, then soon into Queen's Wood, looping through to continue into Highgate Wood. It's then back on the rail line and up to Muswell Hill. Through a small green space (The Grove), you're then climbing up to Alexandra Palace for a short stretch then down through the park to Alexandra Palace station.

FINSBURY PARK TO ALLY PALLY

A. Turn right at the Corporation board (above) continuing on the Capital Ring
B. Head straight on at a crossroads following sign for 'Café & Toilets'
C. Ignore left turn and continue to a T-junction. Follow the Capital Ring sign that directs you right
D. Continue following Capital Ring signs as you bear left at stone fountain to arrive at a gate that you ignore. Turn right (leaving the Capital Ring) and head along the path to the Cranley Gate
E. Exit the woods and turn left up road

A. Head up Muswell Hill Road – take ramp on your left (above) downwards
B. Follow path as it cuts back under the road. Continue on along the ex-railway again, taking the underpass at the end beneath Muswell Hill Road

ALEXANDRA PALACE

THE GROVE

ALEXAND

MUSWELL HILL PARK ROAD

MUSWELL HILL RD

HIGHGATE WOOD

CAFE QUEEN'S WOOD

ARCHWAY RD

Highgate

QUEENS WOOD ROAD

PRIORY GARDENS

HIGHGATE LIBRARY

SHEPHERD'S HILL

HOLMESDALE RD

NORTHWOOD ROAD

STANHOPE RD

A. In Queen's Wood, take a left at the first fork up a stepped path (above)
B. Follow Capital Ring signs through the woods, crossing over Queen's Wood Road
C. Continue on following the Capital Ring signs (Ignore a sign for 'Park Road & Hornsey')
D. Follow a sign for 'Muswell Hill Road & Highgate Wood' – head past the cafe to arrive at Muswell Hill Road. Use the crossing and enter Highgate Wood

A. Cross over towards the station, then turn right along Shepherd's Hill
B. 30 metres on head left through a gap into woods (before Highgate Library)
C. Follow the path straight ahead to emerge onto Priory Gardens – turn right
D. As the road starts to curve take a signposted left path (above) down steps into Queen's Wood

A. The path forks – head up left and through the gate onto Holmesdale Road (above) and turn right up the hill
B. Turn right at the top along Archway Road, heading towards Highgate station (Tube sign visible in front of you)

A. Head right along the road until you arrive at a green metal fence (on right)
B. Look for the sign for the station (above) and turn down the path to reach the end

RK

A. After the underpass take the covered pathway (above) into The Grove
B. Follow the path left around the building and along a tree lined avenue
C. The path turns left at the end of the straight - bear right on the path past a white metal vehicle access gate
D. Follow path down to the road, cross over and head up left to the Palm Court Entrance of Alexandra Palace

A. Turn right in front of the entrance (above) and circle around the Palace
B. Take the first set of steps down to the road (on right). Cross the road and continue down. Take first gravel path on left
C. The path turns left - drop onto tarmac path to right and continue in same direction
D. Take the first right (tarmac path). Heading back on yourself, turn left along a golden gravel path
E. At a fork take the right path - follow it until you reach the road

FINISH
⇒ Alexandra Palace

A. Leave Finsbury Park station by the 'Strand Green Road' exit. Take the pedestrian crossing and enter Finsbury Park next to the cycle sign (above)
B. Follow path around past building and take the first left (gravel path)
C. Head alongside the train line to the top of the path. Turn left and cross the railway footbridge following a Capital Ring sign 'Highgate 2m'

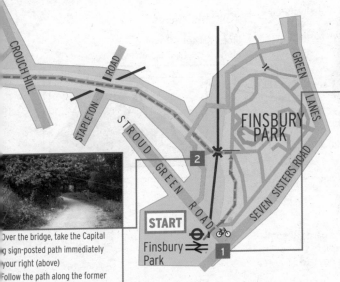

FINSBURY PARK

CROUCH HILL

STAPLETON ROAD

STROUD GREEN ROAD

GREEN LANES

SEVEN SISTERS ROAD

START
Finsbury Park ⇒

Over the bridge, take the Capital ...g sign-posted path immediately ...your right (above)
...Follow the path along the former ...way line for approx. 1.5 miles

FINSBURY PARK TO ALLY PALLY

Getting there

Finsbury Park station is an overland and Tube interchange. It's on both the Piccadilly and Victoria lines.

The overground service runs from, amongst others, Moorgate and King's Cross St Pancras (5 mins journey time).

Please note that at the time of going to press, the station is being remodelled and exits may change.

Alexandra Palace is 6 minutes from Finsbury Park station on trains heading towards Moorgate.

Finsbury Park is in Zone 2 and Alexandra Palace in Zone 3.

Opening Times

Finsbury Park (the green space, not the Tube station) is open from 08.00 until dusk each day. If you are planning to run in winter it's worth checking the closing time with the council – parkscustomercare@haringey.gov.uk.

Useful links and other info

The route is mostly in the Borough of Haringey (www.haringey.gov.uk) but a little bit of the Parkland Walk is in Islington (www.islington.gov.uk)

The Capital Ring is one of the Greater London Authority's Strategic Walking Routes. The TFL website has some details on the Capital Ring and you can also order leaflets on the route: (www.tfl.gov.uk/streets/walking/home.shtml).

The route follows part of sections 11 and 12 of the Ring.

Alexandra Palace has it's own website - www.alexandrapalace.com.

Signs and maps

Finsbury Park has information boards at some entrances. We've mentioned where you're following the Capital Ring and need to rely on the signs.

Refreshments

There are plenty of shops near Finsbury Park station. En route, there are shops around Highgate station. There aren't any convenient shops at the top end near Alexandra Palace station.

Toilets

There are toilets at Finsbury Park station (on platforms 1/2). Also in Finsbury Park (not en route) and in HIghgate Wood (follow signs).

Parking

Parking available in Finsbury Park itself (pay and display - 50p for two hours).

Bike parking

There is a bike parking facility owned by Transport for London just opposite Finsbury Park station on Stroud Green. It's slightly complicated – you've got to fill in a form and get your bike photographed and get a swipe card – but it's secure and worth it if you're going to be a regular user. See www.tfl.gov.uk/cycles/projects/howtouse-cycle-parking.shtml for details.

Hills and climbs

Total ascent 137 metres
Total descent 126 metres

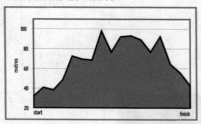

A green and pleasant hilly 5-mile loop around the parks of Brent Cross and Hendon and back along the banks of the Dollis Brook

NORTHERN EXPLORER - BRENT CROSS LOOP

Not a shopping centre in sight

Brent Cross is probably best known for it's shopping centre, which claims to be the oldest of it's kind in the UK. We've managed to find a run that steers clear of the heaving masses.

This is the first of our Explorer routes in the book - taking in several smaller green spaces linked together by quieter roads and paths to produce a run that's a lot more than the sum of its parts. This route takes in both Hendon Park and Sunny Hill Park as you're heading north; on the return journey there's a stretch along the Dollis Brook, one of the tributaries of the River Brent, which in turn feeds the Thames. It's a pretty little stream at this point, quite different to running along the Thames Path.

You also head through Brent Park, alongside former duck decoy ponds, once used to catch wild birds for food. Given the proximity to the North Circular, there's still a surprising number of wildfowl on the waters and it feels well-removed from the rushing traffic just nearby. In total, the route is more than two thirds green spaces and footpaths - pretty fantastic given the urban density of the local area.

Overall, it's at least as rewarding as an hour of retail therapy.

KEY FACTS

🏃	5.0 miles / 8.0 kms
🔁	Loop
🌳	Parks, paths, stream-side paths and roads
START FINISH	Brent Cross Tube station
🕐	Unrestricted
↔	Fairly easy
👟	Mostly hard pavements - one section of grass only running
🏃🏃	Pretty quiet
⛰	Hilly
🚗	Several short road sections, several road crossings (main ones are pedestrianised)
🚻	None
P	At station
🚲	At station
☕	At station

THE ROUTE

From Brent Cross station a couple of streets take you down to a footbridge to get over the North Circular Road. Then head through Hendon Park to pick up the long footpath heading for Church Road. At the top, a short road section takes you to your second green space, Sunny Hill Park. Pass through the park and then over the A1 footbridge - a quick wiggle past Hendon Rugby Club pitches and along a couple of minor roads takes you down to join up with the Dollis Brook. You follow the brook south along it's banks and then through Brent Park. A final short road section takes you back to the station.

NORTHERN EXPLORER - BRENT CROSS LOOP

6

A. Head up into the park (above). Follow the tarmac path, tracing the park's left hand perimeter
B. At tarmac T-junction turn right uphill (across the middle of the park)
C. Continue on to a park entrance (road on the right). Head down left to where several paths meet, then take the path up the other side of the park along the fence on right
D. Continue straight on, then around to the right and up to the main road

4

A. At the top, leave the park and cross straight over the road into West View Path opposite (above), signposted 'Footpath leading to Church Road'
B. Head all the way along the footpath ignoring left and right branches. Towards the end bear left behind shops to arrive at the main road (Claddagh Ring pub opposite)

5

A. Take the zebra crossing to the left and then head into the road in front of you (Church End)
B. Continue past the Chequers pub, the church and the Greyhound pub
C. You begin to head downhill - 30 metres on take a slightly hidden right into Sunny Hill Park

3

A. Head along the path with the train line on the left. At the first fork head right, then across the first junction (Capital Ring sign with tube logo directs you)
B. Head up to a stone drinking fountain. Continue uphill along path with houses on right and sports pitches on left

2

A. Over the bridge turn immediately right (small 'shopping centre' sign directs you), then right again up to and past Clive Lodge (sign on building)
B. Head alongside the rail arches up to the road. Turn right under the rail line and follow the road as it curves around
C. Cross over and enter Hendon Park through the gate (above)

1

A. Leave Brent Cross station by the 'Highfield Avenue, Hendon Way' exit and head up to the road
B. Turn left, then left again into Heathfield Gardens. Head up and over hill (past the other Tube station exit)
C. Arrive at the North Circular - turn left and head over using the footbridge (above)

7

A. Exit the park. Turn right, then up and over the footbridge over the A1 (above)
B. Take the steps down the other side (not the ramp) and head straight forward along Greenlands Lane through the green metal gates

8

A. Turn immediately right before the rugby club building. Head along the grass between the fence and pitches (above)
B. Head through a gap in the hedge at the end to reach the allotments access road. Turn right up to the main road
C. Turn left along the main road for 200m, then take the first left into Ashley Lane (Ashley Court at top of road)
D. Turn first right into Manor Hall Avenue

9

A. Follow the road to the end. Turn left, cross the road and take the first right into Holders Hill Crescent
B. As the road bends right, cross over and take the footpath (signposted 'Footpath leading to Wickliffe Avenue')

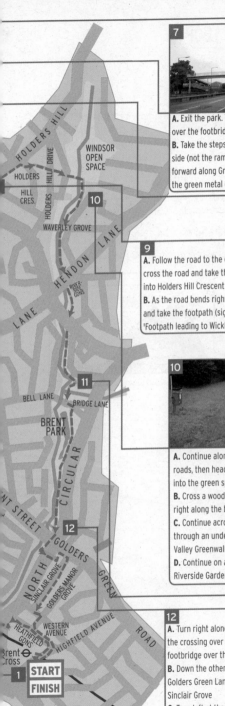

10

A. Continue along the footpath over two roads, then head straight on along path into the green space (above)
B. Cross a wooden bridge, then turn right along the banks of Dollis Brook
C. Continue across first road and then through an underpass (signed 'Dollis Valley Greenwalk')
D. Continue on along the path past Riverside Gardens (on left)

11

A. The path bears right to run alongside a green space. Continue straight on (above) over the bridge and along to Bridge Lane
B. Turn left, cross the road and then right through gate into Brent Park
C. Head straight on to the end of the pond (on right), then straight on along middle of three paths
D. Continue on along the path with the Dollis on your right. At the end head up left to the main road (not right over the green footbridge)

12

A. Turn right along main road. Take the crossing over Brent Road, then the footbridge over the main road
B. Down the other side, head along Golders Green Lane, then first right into Sinclair Grove
C. Turn left at the top, then right, left and right to arrive back at the station

NORTHERN EXPLORER – BRENT CROSS LOOP

Getting there

The route starts at Brent Cross Tube station, which is in Zone 3 on the Edgeware Branch of the Northern Line.

There are 2 exits to Brent Cross Tube station. We've used the main exit – the other one is slightly more logical (you pass it on the route) – but it's closed on Sundays.

Opening Times

This route is not restricted by specific opening times.

Useful links and other info

Hendon Park and Sunny Hill Park are in the Borough of Barnet (www.barnet.gov.uk). Brent Park is in Brent (www.brent.gov.uk). Both sites have some information on the parks in their area (albeit limited).

The Dollis Brook Greenwalk path forms part of the London Loop walk (Section 16 Elstree to Cockfosters). You can get a leaflet on this from the Transport For London website (www.tfl.gov.uk/streets/walking/home.shtml).

Signs and maps

The route is fairly well signposted along the footpaths and along the Dollis Valley Greenwalk.

Refreshments

There is a newsagent at the station where you can pick up a drink and snack. After that there are shops just near Church Road at the end of the footpath in 5.

Toilets

There are no toilets en route or at the station.

Parking

There is a limited amount of parking available at the station - it's really commuter parking, so you're paying by the day during the week (£3), £1 on Saturday and free on Sundays.

Bike parking

Bike parking is limited – there are two bike rails outside the main entrance to the station.

Hills and climbs

Total ascent/descent 88 metres

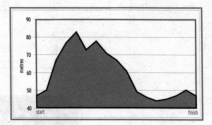

A 5-mile loop along the banks for the Lee and around the wilds of Walthamstow Marshes

WALTHAMSTOW MARSHES & THE RIVER LEE

Flying around the Marshes

Combining the open spaces of Walthamstow Marshes with long quiet river stretches makes this route great for a late summer evening.

The opening section along the River Lee (or Lea depending on which map you look at) is a semi-suburban, semi-industrial start to the run. Along the banks there's still evidence of its working past in the warehouses and cranes leaning out over the water. There's also plenty of pleasure boat traffic up and down the river, especially around Springfield Marina, which you pass en route.

Walthamstow Marshes was the site of some of the earliest powered flights in Britain, being used by aircraft pioneer AV Roe as a testing ground. It's got decent paths throughout most of it but thankfully remains undeveloped giving it a slightly wild feel in places.

It's also one of the few remaining wetland habitats in London and a Site of Special Scientific Interest to boot. So if you're into Essex Skipper butterflies or willow warblers, this is for you.

And allegedly the mythical big cat, the Beast of Ongar, comes down this far. You have been warned...

KEY FACTS

	5 miles / 8 kms
	Loop
	Riverside towpaths and marshes
START FINISH	Tottenham Hale Tube/overland station
	Unrestricted
	Easy. Only one tricky bit across Leyton Marsh
	Mostly hard surfaces NOT PASSABLE FOLLOWING HEAVY RAIN LOW BRIDGE HAZARDS
	Pretty quiet
	Pretty flat
	One very short road section at start/end
	At station
P	At station
	At station
	At station

THE ROUTE

From Tottenham Hale station it's a short road stretch to join up with the River Lee, then south along the towpath down to Springfield Marina. Shortly after you swap banks and continue along the river beside Walthamstow Marshes towards Lee Bridge. At King's Bridge, turn your back on the river and head through Leyton Marsh, then up along the Marshes cycle path to Copper Mill Fields. Heading back towards the Lee, a quick jog through Springfield Marina brings you back over High Bridge - you then retrace your steps back on the towpath to the station.

WALTHAMSTOW MARSHES & THE RIVER LEE

START
FINISH

Tottenham
Hale

FERRY LANE

1

2

JARROW ROAD

REEDHAM CLOSE

WALMEAD ROAD

RIVER LEE

MARKFIELD
RECREATION
GROUND

3

RESERVOIR

10

HIGH
BRIDGE

COPPERMILL
BRIDGE

4

SPRINGFIELD
MARINA

11

SPRING HILL

HORSE SHOE
BRIDGE

5

SPRINGFIELD
PARK

CLAPTON COMMON

SPRINGFIELD

BIG HILL

1

Subway to
Ferry Lane (south)

A. From Tottenham Hale station, take
the Subway under Ferry Lane (above)
B. You emerge from the subway facing
Ferry Road and the station - turn right
so you immediately cross the bridge
over the railway line

2

A. You take a crossing over the top of
Jarrow Road (on your right)
B. Before you cross the bridge, take the
ramp on right down to the towpath (above)

3

A. At the bottom of the ramp head
straight on along the towpath (above)
B. You head under two rail bridges
and past a park (Markfield Recreation
Ground)

4

A. You arrive at Springfield Marina,
with the High Bridge (above) in front
of you
B. Continue under the bridge on the
towpath past Springfield Park (on right)

5

A. At Horseshoe Bridge (above) - cross
the Lee over to the Marshes
B. Over the bridge turn right and take
the path along the other bank of the Lee
(Walthamstow Marshes on your left)

A. Head into the Marina past the entrance sign and follow the path over a bridge
B. Take the path alongside black metal fence and over High Bridge in front of you (above)
C. Over the bridge, turn right and retrace your steps along the Lee to the station

Low bridge and water hazard

This route has an extremely low bridge just after Coppermill Fields Car Park. At just 5 feet (barely 1.5 metres) it's fine for dogs and most short cows.

There is flooding under this bridge after heavy rain – if it's been very damp we'd recommend you chose a different route or prepare to get quite wet.

A. You pass through Coppermill Field car park - turn immediately left and pass under a very low bridge (above) - duck!
B. Continue along path through the gate ahead to the Marina

A. As you arrive at the railway bridges, take the underpass down to the right (above)
B. Pass under both rail lines and through a gate on the other side – continue along path

A. At the top of the path turn left and head straight along a wide cycle path (above)

A. Follow a wooden sign for 'Waterworks Visitor Centre, Lea Valley Riding Centre' heading into the open marsh (above)
B. Head forwards and right towards lampposts on the far side. On the other side continue up a fence-lined tarmac path

OPPERMILL
ELDS

WALTHAMSTOW
MARSH
NATURE
RESERVE

RIVER LEE

RIDING SCHOOL

LEYTON MARSH

KINGS HEAD BRIDGE

LEA VALLEY ICE CENTRE

LEA BRIDGE ROAD

A. You continue along the Lee under a rail bridge. King's Head Bridge (above) comes into view
B. Don't take the bridge - turn left opposite it into the Marshes

WALTHAMSTOW MARSHES & THE RIVER LEE

Getting there

You start and finish at Tottenham Hale Tube/overland station.

There is a reasonable overland service, typically 4 trains per hour during the week and 2 per hour on Sundays. Trains are out of Liverpool Street towards Cambridge or Hertford East and the journey time is around 12 minutes.

Tottenham Hale is on the Victoria Line in Zone 3.

Opening Times

The route doesn't pass through any areas affected by specific opening times.

Useful links and other info

The River Lee and Walthamstow Marshes are looked after by the Lee Valley Regional Park Authority - see their website for more details (www.leevalleypark.org.uk).

The British Waterways site gives details of towpath closures on canals and rivers - it's worth checking their site before you set out www.waterscape.com/boating/stoppages/.

Signs and maps

Walthamstow Marshes are fairly well signposted and there are interesting information boards around too. The one tricky bit on the route is across Leyton Marsh - unfortunately difficult to signpost - you've just got to set off across the marsh in the general direction the sign points you.

Refreshments

There's a kiosk at Tottenham Hale station. If that's shut then there are fast food places and a service station just nearby.

Toilets

There are toilets at Tottenham Hale station on the overland platforms.

Parking

There is pay and display parking at Tottenham Hale station. It's £3.50 per day Monday to Friday and £1 at the weekends and bank holidays.

Bike parking

There are bike racks at the station.

Hills and climbs

Total ascent/descent 19 metres

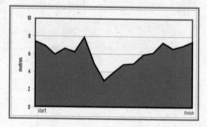

A 4-mile taster around the Heath, taking in Kenwood House and Highgate Cemetery. Steep climbs and great views

HAMPSTEAD HEATH & HIGHGATE

A classic we couldn't leave out

The tracks around Hampstead are worn thin from the foot traffic that passes this way. But it'd be remiss to do a Zones 1 – 3 book and not include 'The Heath'. So, this is pleasant if tough taster of what's on offer for those of us who aren't too familiar with this part of London or locals who want to try a slightly different route.

Famous for spots like Parliament Hill, the ponds and Kenwood House, it's charm really lies in the fact that it's not overly well-kempt. There are masses of tracks and trails criss-crossing through woods and open areas. Some are official, others are just well-worn short cuts – it's often impossible to tell the difference between the two.

We've tried to come up with a route that's relatively easy to follow (for Hampstead Heath) but it does require a bit of diligence and close attention to the directions.

For a bit of variety we also head up to Highgate Village past the Cemetery. One of the Magnificent Seven Great London Cemeteries, it's probably most famous for being the final resting place of Karl Marx. We'd strongly recommend taking a trip back there and getting on one of the guided tours if you want a proper look around – it's well worth it.

KEY FACTS

🏃	4.2 miles / 6.7 kms
↻	Loop
🌳	Heath, roads, parkland, cemetery and a grand house
START FINISH	Hampstead Heath overland station
🕐	Restricted (Kenwood House grounds)
⟷	Very difficult
👟	Mixed – mostly hard paths and trails
👫	Lots of people
⛰	Very hilly
🚗	Some road running – some crossings (mostly using pedestrianised crossings)
🚻	En route
P	Near start
🚲	At station
🍺	Nearby

THE ROUTE

From Hampstead Heath station you're heading away from the bustle of the main road up South Hill Park and quickly into The Heath for the first time. A short section takes you to the Highgate side and from there you climb up Swain's Lane past the Cemetery, nipping through Waterlow Park and up to the village. You then drop down back into The Heath and through the grounds of Kenwood House, before heading back into the Heath proper and up to Parliament Hill summit. You then leave the Heath and it's a short road section back to the station.

HAMPSTEAD HEATH & HIGHGATE

8
A. Continue on along the path straight past the front of the house
B. The path bears left, continue to follow it alongside a metal fence, then beside the lawns and down to a junction at the corner of the lake

7
A. The path weaves around to arrive at a crossroads. Go straight on through the Highgate Gate into Kenwood (information board inside gate confirms your location)
B. Take the path right and follow it straight on, ignoring a left turn. Emerge into an open space (lake on left)
C. Continue up on the same path. Kenwood House (above) appears ahead - continue along the path up to it

6
A. Follow path straight on between two ponds and around to the right along a metal fence on your right
B. At the end of the fence there are three paths - take the middle one (above) up into the trees

9
A. Turn right down a path (above) and over a brick bridge
B. Follow the path right between several huge trees and straight on beside a wire mesh fence (on right)
C. Just past the Great Storm Monument (square stone on right of path), bear right to follow path to the Hampstead Gate (ignore wooden double gate on right)

10
A. Leave the Kenwood grounds via the Hampstead Gate. Take the second path from the left (above)
B. Keep heading along the same path. Emerge into an open section - continue forward. At the second of two wooden posts in the path, head straight forward taking the right hand one of two paths that head into the woods again
C. Path runs alongside another (on left), then curves right to a junction (no cycling sign on footpath). Head straight on past another no cycling sign and follow tarmac path as it heads around right

11
A. You emerge from bushes. Take the next left (above) up to the top of Parliament Hill to take in the views
B. Turn around and back down the path you just came up but take the first left down to the road (Parliament Hill)
C. Follow the road all the way along and retrace your steps to the station

HAMPSTEAD LANE

KENWOOD HOUSE

8

9

KENWOOD

HIGHGATE GATE

7

SPANIARDS ROAD

HAMPSTEAD GATE

10

HAMPSTI

HEAT

VALE OF HEALTH

HEATH STREET

HAMPSTEAD PONDS

SOUTH HILL PARK

SOUTH END ROAD

1

START FINISH

Hampste
Hea

A. Opposite Pond Square at the top (toilets in front of you), turn left and head down South Grove

B. Continue into Highgate West. Take the zebra crossing and continue downhill (be careful on this narrow path)

C. Take first right down Merton Lane - head all the way to the end and re-enter the Heath (above)

A. Continue up Swain's Lane as it bears left and alongside the East Cemetery

B. Just past the main cemetery gates - turn right into Waterlow Park (above), then immediately left to take the path that traces the perimeter of the park

C. Follow path up to an exit (next to tennis courts) - leave the park and turn right continuing up Swain's Lane again

A. Exit the Heath. Turn left up Highgate Road and at the zebra crossing (above) cross the road towards the Duke of St Albans pub

B. Head around the pub and up Swain's Lane

A. Enter the Heath through gate at the end of Nassington Road (above)

B. Head forward along the path (building on right). Bear left past the children's play area and running track. Continue straight on past the bandstand, cafe and tennis courts and down to the road

A. With your back to the main road, head up South Hill Park past station (above)

B. At first fork head right along Parliament Hill, then take next right into Nassington Road. Follow this road all the way down to the Heath

Navigation Tip

Parliament Hill refers not only to the summit itself but also one of the roads leading up from the station directly to Hampstead Heath. Be careful with the directions - we've tried to make it clear which of these were referring to in the text.

Once you're up there the views down towards the centre of London (and beyond) are pretty spectacular...

Map labels: HIGHGATE HIGH STREET, SOUTH GROVE, HIGHGATE WEST, MERTON LANE, TENNIS COURTS, WATERLOW PARK, HIGHGATE CEMETERY WEST, HIGHGATE CEMETERY EAST, HIGHGATE PONDS, SWAIN'S LANE, Duke Of St Albans, HIGHGATE ROAD, TENNIS COURTS, PARLIAMENT HILL, BANDSTAND

HAMPSTEAD HEATH & HIGHGATE

Getting there

The route starts at Hampstead Heath overland station, which is in Zone 3.

It's on the Silverlink North London Line that runs between Stratford/North Woolwich in the east and Richmond in the west (there isn't a Central London Terminus). Usually 4 trains per hour and 2 per hour at weekends. We'd recommend using the Transport For London Journey Planner if you're coming out of Central London (www.tfl.gov.uk).

Opening Times

Access to The Heath isn't restricted but the grounds of Kenwood House are closed during the hours of darkness. Typically this means it's open as follows:

April to October: 08.00 to 20.30
November to March: 08.00 to 16.45

Specific gates will close earlier than this. If you're in the grounds near these times then make sure you get out in good time.

Waterlow Park is open from 07.00 to dusk each day.

Useful links and other info

Hampstead Heath is managed by The City of London (www.cityoflondon.gov.uk). Their website has comprehensive information on The Heath. There are downloadable maps and guides to running and getting started as a runner on Hampstead Heath. If only every council site was this useful for runners.

Kenwood House is looked after by English Heritage – both the house and the grounds are free to visit. The summer concerts (classics and light-ish pop) are well known. See their website (www.english-heritage.org.uk) for details.

If you want to visit rather than just run past Highgate Cemetery then a visit to the Friends of Highgate Cemetery website is in order – (www.highgate-cemetery.org)

Waterlow Park is managed by the Borough of Camden (www.camden.gov.uk). Check the site for up to date opening times.

Signs and maps

There are good information boards around the entrances to both The Heath and Kenwood but once away from the edges it can get tricky, even with a map. Do prepare yourself for the likelihood that you might get a little lost if it's your first visit.

Refreshments

There are plenty of shops near the station at the start of the route.

Toilets

None at the station. En route, there are toilets near the Staff Yard in Hampstead Heath (just before the tennis courts mentioned in 2B) and on re-entering the Heath (5C). Also at the top of Swain's Lane in Pond Square.

Parking

There is metered parking near the start and the City of London website has guidance on parking in and around Hampstead Heath.

Bike parking

There are bike racks on the eastbound platform (it's down some steps).

Hills and climbs

Total ascent/ descent 133 metres

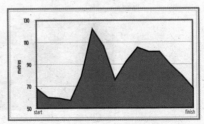

A varied 4.3 mile loop linking three of South East London's smaller parks with a great cemetery and taking in one of London's 'other' rivers

SOUTHERN EXPLORER – THE CATFORD LOOP

There's more to Catford than the South Circular

Catford isn't well known as a running spot, but we think this route is worth heading down south for.

We've linked together several smaller green spaces giving a good mix of short climbs and stretches on the flat.

Blythe Hill Fields are tucked away in a residential area. The short climb to the top offers great views across to Canary Wharf and the infamous Gherkin rising above the City.

The section through Brockley and Ladywell cemeteries is nice and quiet – whilst not one of the Magnificent Seven, it's still atmospheric and peaceful. If you're squeamish about running through a graveyard then you can stick to the footpaths around Ivy Lane and rejoin the route for the climb up to Hill Fields.

A lovely meander along the banks of the Ravensbourne River takes you past Catford Greyhound Stadium, closed since 2003. You can still see the name over the old entrance as you head back to the start.

The lack of traffic throughout most of this route makes for a surprisingly quiet and green route, less than half an hour out of central London.

	KEY FACTS
🏃	4.1 miles / 6.6 kms
🔄	Loop
🏞	Roads, parks, hills and a cemetery
START FINISH	Catford or Catford Bridge overland station
🕐	Restricted
↔	Fairly easy – a bit tricky through the cemetery
👟	Mixed – tarmac pavement on roads, solid paths or grass options in the parks
👥	Pretty quiet
⛰	Hilly
🚗	There is some road running along main roads – others are fairly quiet. Several crossings
🚻	At station (limited access)
P	Near station
🚲	At station
☕	Near start and en route

THE ROUTE

From just outside Catford station head away from the South Circular up Ravensbourne Road. Several roads later, head into the first park - Blythe Hill Fields, then drop down past Crofton Park station. After a short stretch along Brockley Road enter Brockley & Ladywell Cemeteries and loop through from one gate to the other. Complete another little road wiggle and climb into Hilly Fields heading past the Prendergast School. Back on the road again, head for Ladywell Fields, then track the Ravensbourne River through the parkland. A final short road stretch takes you back to the station.

SOUTHERN EXPLORER - THE CATFORD LOOP

3

A. Continue to the end of Crofton Park Road and cross over Brockley Grove into Marnock Road (one way)
B. Head past Crofton Park station platforms (on right through the fence)
C. At the top of the road turn right past the front of the station (above) along Brockley Road. Continue along the main past the library. Brockley Cemetery appears on your right through railings

4

A. Enter Brockley and Ladywell Cemeteries through gates on corner of Ivy Road - take path immediately left
B. Path curves right - turn left at end
C. Next junction - left
D. Next junction - left. Head on towards the chapel (roof visible in front of you) and pass under the chapel porch (above)
E. Head up to roundabout and continue forwards to the entrance gate
F. Turn immediately left up Ivy Road (cemetery wall on left)
G. Turn right into St Cyprian's Path (sign for 'Brockley & Lewisham College')

2

A. Turn right and cross over, then shortly take the footpath (above) up into Blythe Hill Fields
B. At the top of the hill the path splits - head right and down towards a park entrance onto a road with a sharp bend
C. Leave the park, turn right and follow the road (Codrington Hill) around to the junction
D. Cross over into Crofton Park Road and continue straight on (the road bends around to the left)

1

A. Start from the corner of Catford Road and Ravensbourne Park (just outside Catford station)
B. Turn your back on the main road and head under the rail bridge (above) up Ravensbourne Park
C. Cross road and take first left up Ravensbourne Park Crescent
D. When the Crescent turns right don't follow it - head straight on into Casslee Road and up to the top

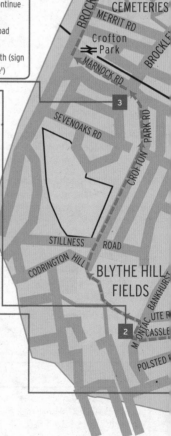

ALTERNATIVE ROUTE AVOIDING CEMETERY

BROCKLEY & LADYWELL CEMETERIES

BROCKLEY ROAD

IVY ROAD

MERRIT RD

Crofton Park

MARNOCK RD

CROFTON PARK RD

SEVENOAKS RD

STILLNESS ROAD

CODRINGTON HILL

BLYTHE HILL FIELDS

BANKHURST

MONTACUTE R

CASSLEE

POLSTED R

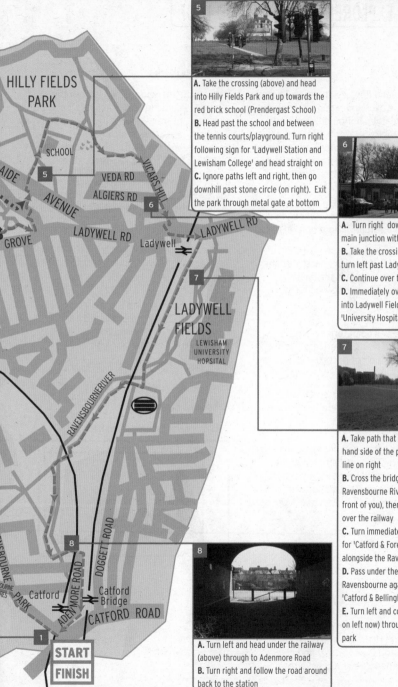

HILLY FIELDS PARK

SCHOOL

LAIDE

5

VEDA RD

ALGIERS RD

AVENUE

VICARS HILL

6

GROVE

LADYWELL RD

LADYWELL RD

Ladywell

7

LADYWELL FIELDS

LEWISHAM UNIVERSITY HOSPITAL

RAVENSBOURNE RIVER

8

DOGGETT ROAD

RAVENSBOURNE PARK

BOURNE CRES

ADENMORE ROAD

Catford

Catford Bridge

CATFORD ROAD

1

START FINISH

A. Take the crossing (above) and head into Hilly Fields Park and up towards the red brick school (Prendergast School)
B. Head past the school and between the tennis courts/playground. Turn right following sign for 'Ladywell Station and Lewisham College' and head straight on
C. Ignore paths left and right, then go downhill past stone circle (on right). Exit the park through metal gate at bottom

A. Turn right down Vicars Hill to the main junction with Ladywell Road
B. Take the crossing to the right, then turn left past Ladywell station (above)
C. Continue over the railway bridge
D. Immediately over the bridge turn right into Ladywell Fields (footpath signposted 'University Hospital Lewisham')

A. Take path that runs down the right hand side of the park (above) - railway line on right
B. Cross the bridge over the Ravensbourne River (running track in front of you), then take the spiral bridge over the railway
C. Turn immediately left following sign for 'Catford & Forest Hill' and continue alongside the Ravensbourne (on right)
D. Pass under the railway, then cross the Ravensbourne again following sign for 'Catford & Bellingham'
E. Turn left and continue on path (river on left now) through to the end of the park

A. Turn left and head under the railway (above) through to Adenmore Road
B. Turn right and follow the road around back to the station

SOUTHERN EXPLORER - THE CATFORD LOOP

Getting there

The route starts and finishes at either Catford or Catford Bridge overland stations. These are next to each other, but on different lines – Blackfriars and Victoria (at the weekends) for Catford, Charing Cross/Waterloo East/London Bridge for Catford Bridge. There are typically 4 trains per hour at peak, fewer on Sundays.

They're both in Zone 3.

If you arrive at Catford Bridge then head up onto bridge and down to Catford station to get to the start.

Crofton Park and Ladywell overland stations, both passed en route, are on the lines to Catford and Catford Bridge respectively.

Opening times

Brockley & Ladywell Cemeteries have restricted opening times. There are people visiting graves, so a bit of decorum is required. Opening times:

March to October: 10.00 to 16.30 daily
November to February: 10.00 to 15.30 daily

Useful links and other info

The route is in the Borough of Lewisham (www.lewisham.gov.uk). Their website has some info on things like cemetery opening times, the parks the route passes through and local parking information.

Signs and maps

There's not much in the way of maps around, and the signage can be confusing. We've referred to the ones you need where they're important for getting around the route.

Refreshments

There are several shops around the stations in Catford. En route there are shops in Brockley Road (near Crofton Park station) and at Ladywell (again near the station).

Other facilities

If you want changing facilities then the Ladywell Fields running track has lockers and showers, not to mention a decent track for a few warm-up (or warm-down) laps. You don't have to be a member to use it. Telephone 020 8314 1986 for more information.

If you do change here then you can join the route at 7B. Or head straight up Doggett Road to get to the stations and the 'official' start.

Toilets

Catford Bridge station has a toilet, although you've got to have a ticket and ask to use it.

Parking

No free parking during the working week (Monday to Friday), but metered parking on Doggett Road and behind the stations on Adenmore Road (80p per hour).

Bike parking

Bike rails outside Catford Bridge station.

Hills and climbs

Total ascent/descent 87 metres

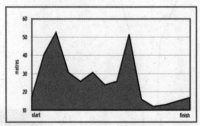

A circular 4-mile loop taking in one of the Magnificent Seven Cemeteries, Peckham Rye Park and a hill where even Queen Elizabeth needed a rest

NUNHEAD CEMETERY & PECKHAM RYE

I ♥ Peckham (and Nunhead)....

Time Out says Nunhead Cemetery is '...possibly the most attractive of the great Victorian cemeteries...'. It's well worth a visit in its own right, as well as having some lovely broad tree-lined tracks that are great for quiet running.

Nunhead is a great example of a cemetery used by locals and visitors alike - you'll find dog walkers and other runners, and the council has added a picnic area, so it's meant to be used.

The recently refurbished Peckham Rye Park has been transformed from a no go area into a great park and a good place for a run. The formal gardens and lake have been restored and you pass both en route.

Aside from that you've got a tough climb up One Tree Hill in Honor Oak. The views into town from the top are a great excuse to pause and get your breath back after the 80-odd steps on the way up. It's also worth visiting the replanted oak tree (just off route) to read the Queen Elizabeth legend.

In our view a great south London run with ample evidence of successful local regeneration.

KEY FACTS

🏃	4.1 miles / 6.6 kms
⇔	Loop
🌳	Roads, parks/gardens and a couple of cemeteries
START FINISH	Nunhead overland station
🕐	Restricted
⬦	Fairly easy
👟	Mixed - tarmac pavement on roads, solid paths or grass options in the parks
👪	Pretty quiet
⛰	Very Hilly
🚗	Some traffic and road crossings
👫	Just off route
P	Nearby
🚲	At station
🍺	Near start and en route

THE ROUTE

A short road section from Nunhead station brings you to the cemetery. Head past the chapel and around the paths to the far gate where you exit for another short road stretch. Cut through Camberwell New Cemetery and climb up the super-steep One Tree Hill for views across south London. Heading down the other side pop through Brenchley Gardens, and then past Camberwell Old Cemetery on Forest Hill Road before entering Peckham Rye Park. You work your way past the formal gardens and around the lake, and then hit the road again back to Nunhead Cemetery and on to the station.

NUNHEAD CEMETERY & PECKHAM RYE

START
FINISH Nunhead

9

8
A. Head left up to the top of Homestall Road. Turn right, cross over and take second left along Stuart Road (past the Ivy House pub)
B. Turn left and head along Borland Road. It merges into Limesford Road (at the junction with Inverton Road) - retrace your steps along Limesford Road back to Nunhead Cemetery

A. Re-enter the cemetery and take the path in front of the gate. Follow it straight back at the Anglican chapel
B. Retrace your steps back to Nunhead station

7

A. Head straight into the park along the path. Take first left
B. Continue on (following signs for the Sexby Garden). At crossroads turn right and head along path (above) past the Sexby Garden (on your left)
C. Take next left, then next right
D. Arrive at the lake and turn left (lake on right). Circle around to a little bridge
E. Take a left over bridge - then second right. Continue on to Homestall Road gate (School/Waverley Sports Centre opposite) and exit park

6

A. Cross over the road and take gate into Brenchley Gardens
B. Work your way left and down to get to the gate in the top right corner (onto Forest Hill Road)
C. Exit onto main road and turn right
D. Continue along road until you arrive at Peckham Rye Park (Elms entrance) immediately on left at top of Colyton Road) - enter the park

30 Great Runs in London

1

A. Exiting Nunhead station, cross carefully and take Oakdale Road (uphill directly opposite the station)
B. Take first right (mini-roundabout) into Linden Grove, signposted for Nunhead Cemetery
C. Take zebra crossing over to opposite side of the road and head through gates into Nunhead Cemetery

Off route

Having slogged up the steps to One Tree Hill it's well worth diverting to see the Oak Tree (there's a plaque on the legend) and head to the viewing point

A. Head straight down the main path to the Anglican chapel (above) and follow the path around to the right
B. At the first fork head left uphill
C. Second fork – head left downhill
D. Follow path as it curves around to the Limesford Road gate. Exit the cemetery and turn right along Limesford Road

A. Take the first left into Inverton Road
B. Continue straight on crossing into Merttins Road (church on corner) and then Brockley Way
C. Turn right into Brenchley Gardens (look for cycle route sign above)
D. Take the pedestrian crossing over the road and enter Camberwell New Cemetery

IVYDALE ROAD

METERY

LIMESFORD RD

ERTON ROAD

MERTTINS ROAD

ATHENLAY ROAD

BROCKLEY WAY

BRENCHLEY GARDENS

CAMBERWELL NEW CEMETERY

CHAPEL

SPORTS GROUND

Honor Oak Park

A. Enter through the main gates and head straight for the chapel (above)
B. Head to the right around the chapel, taking the path that skirts the perimeter of the cemetery (railings and the sports ground on your left)
C. Pass through gate at end of the path into a car park. Bear right diagonally across the car park
D. Head up the car park drive (past allotments on right) and out onto main road (Honor Oak Park)

A. Turn right up Honor Oak Park (past allotments). Take footpath through black gate (above) signposted 'One Tree Hill' and 'St Augustine's Church'
B. Climb the steps - cross the path (church on right) and continue up
C. You arrive at cross roads - viewing point to the left, the oak to your right. Head straight on down path with handrail
D. Follow the path down to the road (ignore gate on left half way down)

NUNHEAD CEMETERY & PECKHAM RYE

Getting there

The route starts and finishes at Nunhead station (Zone 2). The station is served by trains from Victoria (typically 2/3 per hour during the week peak at times and 2 per hour at weekends) – around 15 mins journey time.

The route passes close to Honor Oak station (Zone 3) which is accessible from Charing Cross/Waterloo East/London Bridge. See the TFL website www.tfl.gov.uk for planning your journey.

Turn right out of the station onto Honor Oak Park and pick up the route at 5A.

Opening times

Restricted opening times mean this run can only be done during daylight hours, and after 10.00 on a Sunday.

Nunhead Cemetery opening times:

April to September: 08.00 to 19.00 daily
October to March: 08.00 to one hour before sunset

Camberwell New Cemetery opening times:

April to September: Monday to Saturday 08.00 to 19.00 (from 10.00 on Sundays)

October to March: Monday to Saturday 08.00 to 17.00 (from 10.00 on Sundays)

Peckham Rye Park is open from 08.00 until dusk daily. If you're in there near closing time then check the info boards at the gates for closing times.

Useful links and other info

The route is in the Borough of Southwark (www.southwark.gov.uk). Their website has lots of useful details on the parks and cemeteries.

The Friends of Nunhead Cemetery has it's own website - www.queries.demon.co.uk/fonc. There's lots of pictures to inspire your visit.

The Friends of Peckham Rye Park also have a website - www.foprp.org.uk.

Signs and maps

Peckham Rye Park is well-mapped – look out for the info boards at the park entrances.

Refreshments

There's a decent enough general store just near Nunhead station. En route there are shops along Forest Hill Road and one after you come out of Peckham Rye Park.

Toilets

There aren't any en route, but you'll find some in Peckham Rye Park at the Visitor Centre (follow the signposts in the park).

Parking

It can be tricky around the station - much easier to park (for free) up at the cemetery on Linden Grove. Parking here reduces the distance by half a mile or so.

Bike parking

Bike rails outside Nunhead station. It's a fairly quiet area so make sure it's well secured.

Hills and climbs

Total ascent/descent 103 metres

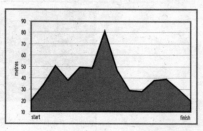

A circular 4.4 mile route around the Rotherhithe peninsula, with fantastic Thames-side running and the surprising Russia Dock Woodland

SURREY QUAYS & ROTHERHITHE

Spectacular riverside running

Rotherhithe feels a little bit off the beaten track. Tucked away in an elbow of the Thames, it's less than a mile from Tower Bridge, just across the water from Wapping and Limehouse and only a stone's throw from the Borough and Bermondsey. So even though it's south of the river, it's easily accessible from the City and Docklands for a lunchtime run.

Starting out in Southwark Park, you head quickly riverside through the historic streets of Rotherhithe, passing the Mayflower pub and Brunel Engine House Museum. The engine house was built for the machinery that drained the first tunnel under the Thames, built by Brunel and opened in 1843. The East London Tube Line still uses the tunnel today.

Further on you're then flanked by residential warehouses and newer developments with great views across to Canary Wharf.

Russia Dock Woodland (a filled in dock that's now a nature reserve) leads on to a tranquil section around the picturesque Greenland Dock.

This route has very little traffic and great varied scenery. Get yourselves out there and discover Rotherhithe.

KEY FACTS

🏃	4.4 miles / 7.0 kms
🔁	Loop
🌳	Formal parkland, riverfront, woodland and dockfront
START FINISH	Surrey Quays Tube station
🕐	Restricted
✥	Quite tricky
👟	Almost all hard surfaces
👥	Pretty quiet
⛰	Flat
🚗	There is some running along roads, but they're mostly quiet. Several crossings, either quiet or pedestrianised
🚻	Off route
P	Near station
🚲	Near station
☕	At station and en route

THE ROUTE

From the Tube station it's quickly into Southwark Park for a gentle start to the run. Head through to the other side then cross the busy Jamaica Road and into King's Stairs Garden to the river front. Head north around the peninsula, sometimes on the river and sometimes in the quiet Rotherhithe streets. Over the top of the peninsula head into Russia Dock Woodlands, and through the paths to arrive at Greenland Dock for the final section, looping around the water front. You then head past Surrey Quays shopping centre to arrive back at the station.

SURREY QUAYS & ROTHERHITHE

5

A. After 30 metres you turn right away from the river, then left following signs for 'Rotherhithe Walk, Village, Station'
B. Continue along a narrow street (above) - past a small Princes House sign on right. Head along the road into Rotherhithe Street, passing the Mayflower pub

6

A. Take a left back to the Thames Path opposite Swan Road. Head past bronze sculpture and along Cumberland Wharf
B. Turn right down steps at the end. Cross the red swing bridge on your left (above) and then turn left in front of the Spice Island pub to continue along the waterside

4

A. Turn right and then take a left following the sign for Cherry Garden (above) to enter King's Stairs Gardens
B. Take the left hand fork, and then head right (around the playground) following the path forward up to the Thames
C. Turn right along the waterfront

3

A. Head all the way along the side of the lake (on left) and continue along the path up to the road (Park Approach)
B. Cross over to the right and re-enter the park on the other side (above) following a sign for 'Bowls Club, Bandstand, Jamaica Rd'
C. Follow the path along the metal fence (on right) past the bowls club (on left)
D. The fence ends - follow the path that bears right up to the Paradise Gate
E. Leave the park and take the two crossings on your left to get over to the other side of Jamaica Road

2

A. Head along Lower Road (to the right of the pub). 20 metres on turn left into Southwark Park through the gates (above)
B. Head right at first junction following sign for 'Lake, Playground Base, WC'
C. At a forked junction with The Gallery in front of you, bear left and then turn right towards the Lake down side of The Gallery

1

A. Leave Surrey Quays station by the exit signposted 'Buses to Bermondsey and London Bridge'
B. Turn right and take the crossings over to the Caulkers Pub (above) on the corner of Lower Road and Hawkstone Road

[Map of Surrey Quays & Rotherhithe area]

RIVER THAMES

Spice Island

KATHERINE CLOSE

SURREY WATER

CUMBERLAND WHARF

BRUNEL ROAD

The Mayflower

ROTHERHITHE STREET

SWAN ROAD

BRUNEL MUSEUM

Rotherhithe

CATHAY STREET

PLAY GROUND

KING'S STAIR GARDENS

TUNNEL APPROACH

Canada Water

SURREY QUAYS ROAD

CANADA WATER

BAND STAND

SURREY QUAY SHOPPING MA

LOWER ROAD

BOWLING GREEN

PARK APPROACH

THE GALLERY

DEAL PORTERS WA

SOUTHWARK PARK

Caulkers

HAWKSTONE ROAD

Surrey Quays

START
FINISH

7

A. Continue along the Thames to Globe Wharf. Turn right away from the river towards Lavender House (sign opposite) and left along Rotherhithe Street

B. Cut back to the riverside at the Three Compasses pub and head along the tree-lined Sovereign Crescent

C. Turn right away from the river again at Canada Wharf, down steps and left along Rotherhithe Street

8

A. You pass the Blacksmiths pub (on left). After the next building cross the road and head up Acorn Walk (above) on your right

B. Turn left before Acorn Walk's gates to enter Pearsons Park

C. Turn immediately right (DON'T go straight on through red gate)

9

A. At first fork head right down and under the road (above)

B. Climb the path bearing to the left, signposted Lavender Dock Walk

10

A. You arrive at a wooden bridge (above) - cross it and follow the path around to the left

B. Turn left over a second wooden bridge (following blue cycle sign for 'Ecopark and Bacon's College')

C. Keep on along the main path (pond on right), then through a gate following sign for 'Bacon's College' again

D. Cross a third wooden bridge and continue straight ahead on the path

11

A. Follow the path ahead as it bears left (above)

B. You then head all the way along a dead straight path through two sets of gates

C. As the path ends, head right down under the road (following signs for Surrey Quays Tube) to reach the Greenland Dock

12

A. Head left and around the dockside in front of the Moby Dick pub to begin circling the dock clockwise (water on right)

B. Cross the Norway Cut Bridge (above), then turn right along the top of the dock across the road bridge (footbridge on left) around to Rainbow Quay

C. Turn right, continuing around the dock (leaving it twice to get around obstacles)

13

A. Continue to the end of the dock and then bear right following sign for the Tube station. Head under the red swing bridge (above) and up the path past Surrey Quays Shopping Centre (on right)

B. Bear left along path after the shopping centre. Two crossings take you back over Lower Road to the Tube station

Navigation tip

Through Russia Dock Woodland the signage is confusing in places. Try to ignore signs not mentioned in the text, otherwise you might end up off route

SURREY QUAYS & ROTHERHITHE

Getting there

The route starts and finishes at Surrey Quays Tube station, which is on the East London Line in Zone 2.

To get to the East London Line take the Jubilee to Canada Water. Surrey Quays is one stop south on the East London Line.

Opening times

Southwark Park is open from 07.30 each day and shuts an hour before dusk. If you're doing the route near sunset then make sure you check the closing times on the information boards at the gates.

Useful links and other info

Southwark Park and Russia Docks are Southwark Council (www.southwark.gov.uk) green spaces. The site is useful for things like parking, access times and contact details.

The Thames Path website can be found at www.nationaltrail.co.uk/thamespath. It's not as useful for runners as it could be, but is a good starting point for information. You can also get Thames Path leaflets from Transport For London (www.tfl.gov.uk/streets/walking/home.shtml).

The Friends of Russia Docks Woodland are active in preserving their green space, their site is www.russiadockwood.ukfriends.com.

En route you pass the Brunel Engine House Museum - worth popping back to after your run (www.brunelenginehouse.org.uk).

Signs and maps

There's decent signage and maps through Southwark Park and around the Thames Path.

The place where you could do with a bit more is through the Russia Dock Woodland - there's room for improvement. Stick to the route and only follow the directions mentioned in the text.

Refreshments

There is a little shop at the Tube station for stocking up - after that it's sparse until you've more or less completed the route. There's a supermarket and other shops in Surrey Quays Shopping Mall.

Toilets

None at the station. There are some in Southwark Park - they aren't quite en route, so follow the signs to find them. Surrey Quays Shopping Mall has toilets too.

Parking

There's three free hours of parking at the shopping mall, although you are meant to be shopping.

There is parking in Southwark Park as well - see the Council's website for details.

Bike parking

There are railings around the Tube station, or more official facilities in Southwark Park near the Hawkstone Road entrance (the Caulkers pub is at the top of Hawkstone Road).

Hills and climbs

There's an almost unnoticable total ascent/descent of just 10 metres on this route.

A great 6-mile straight line route around Crystal Palace Park and through leafy Dulwich

CRYSTAL PALACE & DULWICH VILLAGE

Dinosaurs, sphinxes, Victorian parks and village life

Although there isn't much Victorian splendour left in Crystal Palace Park, the restored dinosaurs and the sphinxes on the Terraces provide an echo of what it must have been like. The difference between Crystal Palace Park and it's northern counterpart Alexandra Palace Park is marked – one still has its palace and is thriving, the other less so.

What to do with the Park has been a matter for debate ever since the Palace burned down in 1936. As it is now, the ruins make for an interesting and atmospheric start to the route.

By contrast, the newly regenerated Dulwich Park is rather spick and span, which seems to suit villagey Dulwich pretty well. And it does show what a bit of municipal determination (and a big slug of Lottery funding) can achieve.

Linking the two is a quiet, undulating road section, passing the last remaining private tollbooth in London and stately Dulwich College.

With plenty of good cafes, pubs and restaurants at both ends of the route, this is a perfect spot for a making your run into a pleasant weekend outing.

KEY FACTS

🏃	6.0 miles / 9.6 kms
⟳	Straight line
	Parks, dinosaurs, roads, village streets (kind of...)
START FINISH	Crystal Palace overland station North Dulwich overland station
🕐	Restricted access to both Crystal Palace and Dulwich Parks
✧	Fairly easy
👟	Mixed – tarmac pavement on roads, solid paths or grass options in the parks
🏃🏃	Quite busy
⛰	Very hilly (although more down than up)
🚗	One short main road section, other road running is fairly quiet. Several crossings
🚻	En route
P	Near station
🚲	At start
🍺	En route

THE ROUTE

From Crystal Palace station head straight into the park and then counter-clockwise around its outer fringes. You soon pass the restored dinosaurs dotted around the lake, and then climb through the park to arrive at the Terraces where the Palace once was. Leaving the park, follow the roads heading down to Dulwich Park past the College and tollbooth. After a loop of the park continue on into Dulwich Village. A short stretch along the high street takes you away from the village centre up to North Dulwich station where the route ends.

CRYSTAL PALACE & DULWICH VILLAGE

THIS IS NOT A PRINTING ERROR

We've turned these pages sideways so we could include a decent sized map and enough information for you to navigate the route

7

A. Continue along College Road past the tollbooth (above) and the grounds of Dulwich College on either side

B. Use the crossing to get you over Dulwich Common – continue straight on

C. Take the zebra crossing in front of Dulwich Picture Gallery and enter into Dulwich Park through the College Gate

6

A. You arrive at a pedestrian crossing (above). Take the crossing over the main road and then again over College Road

B. Turn left and head down College Road

C. Take first right into a one way road (post box on corner), then left to continue down College Road again (past

8

A. Head up the access road and turn left after the vehicle gate (above) onto the playing fields (cycle hire shop and pavilion on left)

B. Circle the playing field clockwise along the perimeter fence

C. At the end of the field (gate and access road on left) head forward onto the main carriage road. Continue to circle the park around to reach the gate you came in by

COURT LANE

DULWICH PARK

LAKE

DULWICH COMMON

8

OLD COLLEGE

GATE

COLLEGE ROAD

DULWICH COLLEGE

9

DULWICH VILLAGE

EAST DULWICH ROAD

North Dulwich

RED POST HILL

10

FINISH

10

A. Continue over the junction at the top of Dulwich Village into Red Post Hill

B. You complete the route at Dulwich North station (above) on the right

9

A. Leave the Park via College Gate and turn right along the road

B. Continue to the right along the main road at the roundabout (above) following the sign for 'North Dulwich Station & Camberwell'

C. Continue up through Dulwich Village (shops and pubs along roadside)

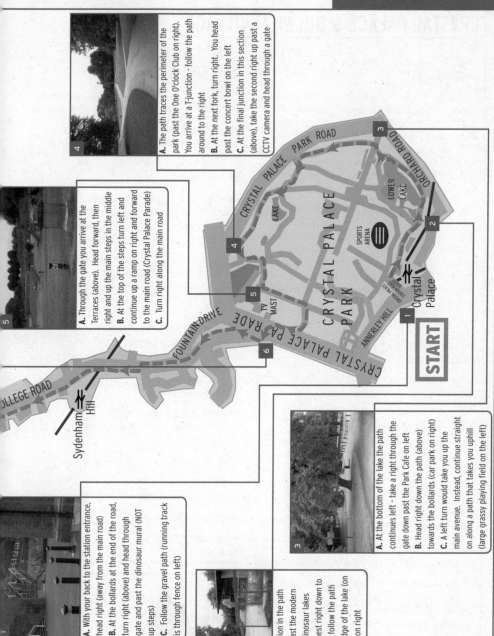

4

A. The path traces the perimeter of the park (past the One O'clock Club on right). You arrive at a T-junction - follow the path around to the right

B. At the next fork, turn right. You head past the concert bowl on the left

C. At the final junction in this section (above), take the second right up past a CCTV camera and head through a gate

5

A. Through the gate you arrive at the Terraces (above). Head forward, then right and up the main steps in the middle

B. At the top of the steps turn left and continue up a ramp on right and forward to the main road (Crystal Palace Parade)

C. Turn right along the main road

6

A. With your back to the station entrance, head right (away from the main road)

B. At the bollards at the end of the road, turn right (above) and head through gate and past the dinosaur mural (NOT up steps)

C. Follow the gravel path (running track is through fence on left)

2

A. You come to a junction in the path (above) - head right past the modern building down to the dinosaur lakes

B. Take the path furthest right down to the lakeside and then follow the path as it runs along the edge of the lake (on left). Ignore exit gate on right

3

A. At the bottom of the lake the path continues left - take a right through the gate down past the Park Cafe on left

B. Head right down the path (above) towards the bollards (car park on right)

C. A left turn would take you up the main avenue. Instead, continue straight on along a path that takes you uphill (large grassy playing field on the left)

CRYSTAL PALACE PARK ROAD

ORCHARD ROAD

LAKE

LOWER LAKE

CRYSTAL PALACE PARK

SPORTS ARENA

TV MAST

FOUNTAIN DRIVE

CRYSTAL PALACE PARADE

OLLEGE ROAD

Sydenham Hill

Crystal Palace

START

ANNERLEY HILL

CRYSTAL PALACE & DULWICH VILLAGE

Getting there

The route starts at Crystal Palace station (Zone 3), which is on the outer South London loop line that runs between Victoria and London Bridge, and also on the West Croydon Line from Victoria. It's typically 20-25 minutes from central London. There is a frequent service with lots of trains during the week and a reasonable weekend service as well.

North Dulwich is on the Zone 2/3 border. There is a good service into London Bridge (14 mins), and services towards Smitham and Beckenham Junction will (usually - check the routing) take you back to Crystal Palace in less than 15 minutes. Note that there's no direct service between North Dulwich and Crystal Palace on Sundays.

Opening times

Both Crystal Palace Park and Dulwich Park are closed at night.

Crystal Palace Park opens at 07.30 each day and closes half an hour before dusk. Some gates may close earlier than this.

In line with other gated Southwark parks, Dulwich Park opens at 08.00 and closes at dusk (between 16.30 and 21.00 depending on the time of year).

Useful links and other info

Crystal Palace Park is in the Borough of Bromley. Their website has a bit on the history of the Park and details of things like parking (www.bromley.gov.uk/leisure/parksandcountryside/crystal_palace_park.htm).

Crystal Palace Park is home to the National Sports Centre. It's operated on behalf of Sport England by Greenwich Leisure. It's possible to get changed there, or even better leave your kit and head back for a swim after your run. See the GL website for details - www.gll.org.

Dulwich Park is in Southwark - for details visit www.southwark.gov.uk.

Signs and maps

Crystal Palace Park isn't very well signposted, and consequently is a bit tricky to get around.

Dulwich Park is well signposted, with good information boards and maps at each of the entrances.

Refreshments

There's not much at either station. At Crystal Palace there are shops just out on the main road (Annerley Hill) and plenty of cafes and restaurants just nearby in Westow Hill.

You pass lots of shops and eating places as you head through Dulwich. There's also refreshment kiosks in both parks, just off route.

Toilets

There are toilets in Crystal Palace Park on the main path near the Park Cafe. There are also toilets in Dulwich Park (as you turn left after entering the park).

Parking

There is free parking in Crystal Palace at the Arena - follow signs to the station to pick up the route.

Bike parking

There are bike parking facilities straight outside Crystal Palace station.

Hills and climbs

Total ascent 82 metres
Total descent 132 metres

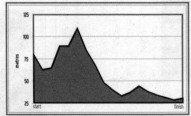

A 7.2-mile loop linking three South West London commons for a varied route

CLAPHAM, TOOTING & WANDSWORTH COMMONS

Uncommonly good common work

Anyone who's driven past Clapham Common early in the morning or after work will have seen the large herds of runners wearing grooves in its perimeter. And that's fine - it's a good-sized green space to make into a regular route. But it hasn't got the most interesting scenery, and so getting a bit further afield can only help keep your running fresh.

And there is a lot more to this corner of London than a circuit of Clapham Common. So, we've devised a route that incorporates two more green spaces linked by roads that aren't the main traffic routes, which should keep your diesel fume intake to a minimum.

Tooting Bec and Wandsworth Commons are actually leafier and greener than their more famous and popular neighbour - this is a good excuse for checking them out.

The route also has plenty of hill work too, which makes it a bit more challenging than the average loop around Clapham Common. Well worth breaking out of the old routine to add some extra distance and a few new sights.

KEY FACTS

🏃	7.2 miles / 11.5 kms
⇔	Loop
🏞	Commons and road
START FINISH	Clapham Common Tube station
🕐	Not restricted
✛	Quite tricky
👟	Mixed - tarmac pavement on roads, solid paths or grass options in the parks
🏃🏃🏃	Quite busy/ Pretty quiet (in places)
⛰	Undulating
🚗	More common than road. Roads are relatively quiet - several crossings
🚻	At start
P	Nearby (tricky)
🚲	At start (see info page)
☕	At start

THE ROUTE

From Clapham Common Tube station head into the Common itself and through the middle towards the bandstand, then down to Clapham South Tube. You wiggle through to get to Cavendish Road and follow this all the way down to Tooting Bec Common. Away from the roads now, head through this green and leafy section of the run to the other end of the Common, where it's back on the road again up to Wandsworth Common. Head through the Common past the ponds and along the railway, then back onto the road again to get back to Clapham Common. Track back past the bandstand to get to the Tube station.

CLAPHAM, TOOTING & WANDSWORTH COMMONS

Shared use paths

Where we refer to 'shared use paths', we mean ones for use by both cyclists and pedestrians generally denoted by white bike/walker signs on the pavement

A. Take the crossing in front (above) - turn right and head diagonally into the Common along the widest path
B. Cross over Rookery Road and head straight on to arrive at a statue, then continue on up to the road
C. Cross over to The Pavement and bear right to the Tube station to complete the route

A. Turn left and head up to the road junction, then right over two crossings (above) to re-enter the Common past a gate
B. Head straight along the tarmac path all the way to the bandstand
C. Circle left and take the first path on left (cafe-bar on right). Cross over the double cycle/pedestrian path and continue on bearing slightly right up to the main road

A. At the top the path bears right then heads out of the Common next to a playground
B. Turn right at the road, then right (above) to take a path back across the Common. Follow path to pedestrian crossing
C. Cross over, turn right then left into Wakehurst Road. Head all the way along the road over several crossroads until Clapham Common is in front of you

A. The shared use path continues on - turn first right along a gravel path (above) towards the pond and playground
B. Cross a stone bridge, then turn immediately left along path that curves around pond. Continue on between the pond and the railway line (on right)
C. Turn right over the footbridge, then left alongside the railway. Head all the way along the path to the top of the Common

A. Turn left along the road and take pedestrian crossing over to the right
B. Head into the Common again on a shared use path (above). Stick to the shared use path - it's joined from the right and bears left over a junction

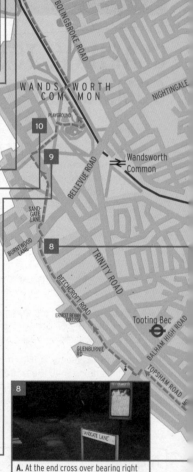

A. At the end cross over bearing right into Sandgate Lane opposite
B. Take the path past the road sign (above). Turn right along trail to head straight across this section of Wandsworth Common to the main road on the other side

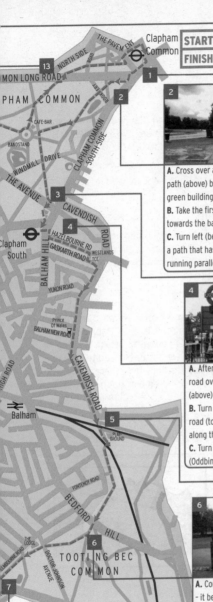

THE PAVEMENT
NORTH SIDE ROAD
Clapham Common
START
FINISH

MON LONG ROAD
13

PHAM COMMON

CAFE-BAR

BANDSTAND

CLAPHAM COMMON SOUTH SIDE

WINDMILL DRIVE

THE AVENUE

3

CAVENDISH

Clapham South

HAZELBOURNE RD
BALHAM HILL
GASKARTH ROAD
WESTLANDS TCE

YUKON ROAD

Prince Of Wales
BALHAM NEW ROAD

CAVENDISH ROAD

IGH ROAD

Balham
5
PLAY GROUND

FONTENOY ROAD

BEDFORD
HILL

THE LODGE

6

TOOTING BEC COMMON
DOCTOR JOHNSON AVENUE
AMBOURNE ROAD

7

1

A. Head out of the Tube following the sign for Clapham Common
B. Turn right and head along the road
C. Cross over the roads in front of you, to arrive in front of the green road sign (above)
D. Head past the sign and take the trail to the right (alongside the road)
E. Turn left along the first tarmac path and follow this down to Rookery Road

2

A. Cross over and continue along the path (above) between the Long Pond and green building
B. Take the first path on right and head towards the bandstand
C. Turn left (before the bandstand) along a path that has a red tarmac cycle path running parallel alongside it on the left

3

A. Continue along to and beyond Windmill Drive. Head straight on along path beside metal railings (on left) – when these end keep straight on to arrive at the road junction (above)
B. Cross over twice (using the island) to continue right into the other part of the Common, where the path heads behind the green buildings

4

A. After the green buildings cross the road over to Clapham South Tube station (above)
B. Turn left and cross over the main road (towards Tesco), and then turn right along the main road
C. Turn first left down Hazelbourne Road (Oddbins on corner)

5

A. Turn first right into Westlands Terrace, then left up to the top of Gaskarth Road
B. Turn right and head along Cavendish Road for approx. 1 km (Prince of Wales pub on right half way along)
C. At the bottom of Cavendish Road head straight on into Tooting Bec Common under the rail bridge (above)
D. Continue straight on (children's play ground on left), then turn right under another rail bridge and continue up path

6

A. Continue to follow the shared use path – it bears around to the right along the perimeter of the Common to arrive at Bedford Hill road
B. Continue straight over (use crossing on left), and along the shared use path (above). Turn right at the first fork (past the cafe)
C. Continue to Dr Johnson Avenue – cross over and head all the way along the path parallel to the road (on right) up to the corner of the Common

7

A. Bear right up to the main road and take the pedestrian crossing over towards Treherne Court
B. Turn right along main road, then left at the Rose & Crown pub up Avoca Road
C. Take the first right (Topsham Road)
D. At the end turn left and take the crossing – then back right and up Beechcroft Road (red church on left)

CLAPHAM, TOOTING & WANDSWORTH COMMONS

Getting there

Clapham Common Tube station is in Zone 2 on the Northern Line.

There are alternative Northern Line starts near to the route – Clapham South is en route (and recommended for cyclists (see below), and Tooting Bec nearby.

For the overland traveller, Balham and Wandsworth Common stations both have frequent services from central London and are near the route.

Opening times

None of the three Commons are closed at night, although we wouldn't recommend running alone along this or any other route in the dark.

Signs and maps

Clapham Common has recently had some new and fairly useful map/info boards installed around it's perimeter. Neither Tooting Bec nor Wandsworth Commons have up to date information boards. None of the three are well signposted once you are actually away from the edges.

Part of the route through Tooting Bec and Wandsworth Common coincide with sections of the Capital Ring. However, the route doesn't follow it closely and so we've not relied on the signposts to guide you through.

Refreshments

There are plenty of shops near Clapham Common station.

Toilets

There are toilets at Clapham Common station. The opening times are currently 08.00 (10.00 on Sundays) until 18.00 (19.00 Thursday and Friday).

After that you've got to head off route to find facilities.

Parking

There is metered parking around Clapham Common Tube station, although it's pretty busy around there and so we don't recommend driving to this route.

Bike parking

Cycle parking is a little awkward around Clapham Common Tube station, although lots of people seem happy to attach their bikes to the railings. Far better to head to Clapham South Tube station where there are lots of bike racks. You can then pick up the run at point 4A on the route.

Hills and climbs

Total ascent/descent 49 metres

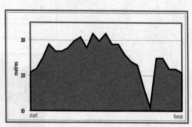

A tough loop comprising a 5-mile circuit of Wimbledon Common and a hill climb to and from the station

WIMBLEDON COMMON

Country-style trail running

Wimbledon Common is in the corner of the map that includes Richmond and Bushey Parks and could be seen as the runt of the litter. It lacks the strong regal connections of the others, and in truth is a little less well-kempt than its neighbours.

So why head to Wimbledon? For a start it's a lot less busy than Richmond – and with better transport connections. But above all it's got what feels more like proper trail running on lovely soft surfaces through wooded paths. Don't get us wrong, Richmond's great, but it's been polished and tweaked to cope with its visitors. Wimbledon hasn't and is all the better for it.

It's a bit of a road trip from the station up to the Common. Whilst it's a good contrast to the greenery to come, you could always do this as a 5-mile loop from the corner of Camp Road (4A), and so if you must take the car then this is probably a better idea than parking near the station. We've marked on the route where the loop starts and ends.

This is a tricky route – the Common isn't well signposted, and the route avoids most of the main paths. But it's well worth persevering for what is a great run.

KEY FACTS

	7.3 miles / 11.7 kms (just a loop of Common is 4.8 miles / 7.6 kms)
	Loop
	Roads and Common trails and paths
START FINISH	Wimbledon Tube/overland/Tramlink station
	Not restricted
	Very difficult
	Mixed – tarmac pavement on roads but some good offroad stuff on the Common VERY WET UNDERFOOT FOLLOWING RAIN
	Quite busy (Pretty quiet in places)
	Very hilly
	There is some road running, mostly along fairly quiet roads. Some crossings
	At station
P	Near station (see info page)
	At station
	At station / en route

THE ROUTE

From the station head quickly away from the high street along a footpath beside the railway line. Then begin the road section, working your way upwards through pleasant suburbs to the start of the Common. Head down past the golf courses to get stuck into the Common proper, arriving at Beverley Brook. Follow the stream for a while and then turn away past Putney Vale Cemetery. Around Jerry's Hill the navigation is tricky, further on continue through the Common on wooded trails, and then head south alongside the road. Eventually arrive back at the roads at the foot of the Common to complete the loop, from where you retrace your steps to the station.

WIMBLEDON COMMON

Shared use paths

By 'shared use path', we mean one designated for use by cyclists and pedestrians – denoted by a small blue sign with a bike and the words 'WITH PEDESTRIAN PRIORITY'

8
A. Keep left along the fringe of the Common (playing fields on left through trees, then a war memorial)
B. A Capital Ring sign points right – bear left and up on the main trail (allotments on left through trees)
C. Continue on (houses through trees on left give way to Putney Vale Cemetery)
D. After passing within a few metres of the cemetery wall continue straight on at a 3-way junction (not left past a no cycling sign). The path then rises steeply

9

A. Continue on to arrive at a pond on your left. You've a choice of 3 paths – head straight on and take path that heads uphill through trees
B. You emerge onto the top of a small hill (above). Head to the right of the young lone oak tree in front of you
C. Follow the path past two more small oaks, and down the other side of the hill past a wooden post (no cycling sign) to a junction

7

A. Just before the next bridge over the brook (sports field in front), take path first right of the one you came along (past a 'Capital Ring/No Cycling' sign)
B. Take narrow path to left (above) and then head up along a wide trail

6

A. At first fork take left hand path and continue forward (ignore paths left and right). Just past concrete fence posts turn left towards a footbridge (above)
B. Turn right and head along trail beside Beverley Brook (on left) for approx. 1 mile (brick bridge half way)

5

A. Head past Eversley Park and Kinsella Gardens. The road ends – take narrow fenced path ahead (golf course on both sides)
B. Follow path to the end (above). Head straight across and take trail to the right ('Beverley Meades Nature Reserve' sign on left in tree)

4

A. Head straight on, to the left of the white house (above) into Camp Road, signposted for the 'Royal Wimbledon Golf Club' (**START OF THE LOOP**)
B. Keep following Camp Road around to the right, and then left as it heads past the golf course (club buildings on left)

KINGSTON ROAD

8

PUTNEY VALE CEMETERY

ROEHAMPTON VALE

STAG RIDE

PLAYING FIELDS

WAR MEMORIAL

7

WIMBLEDON

BEVERLEY BROOK

ROBIN HOOD WAY

HORSE RIDE

ROBIN HOOD ROAD

ROYAL WIMBLEDON GOLF COURSE

BEVERLEY MEADES NATURE RESERVE

5

6

10
A. At the junction, head straight on past a clump of trees to take the wide shared use path straight ahead (above - cycle path sign on right hand side)
B. Continue on the path across the double path (Ladies Mile) that runs crossways and continue towards the road

11
A. You arrive at a bench (above) on the left of the path. There are two small trails opposite on the right
B. Take the left one of these trails into the woods. You cross a hard path - keep heading forward on the other side
C. You join a gravel path - continue straight on, heading past several numbered Windmill Nature Trail way markers. Keep heading forward past a bench to arrive at Windmill Road

12
A. Cross over Windmill Road and turn left along path that runs parallel to the road (above)
B. Follow the path as it bears right and heads down the Common side
C. Continue on along the roadside to the bottom of the Common

13
A. At the bottom turn right along the path that runs alongside Cannizaro Road
B. Turn right alongside the Causeway back up to the corner of Camp Road (**END OF THE LOOP**)
Retrace your steps across the Common and along the roads back to the station

3
A. At the top take Sunnyside Passage and then continue to the end of Sunnyside
B. Cross over road in front of you, turn right, then left up Lingfield Road (church on corner). At top cross over into The Green
C. Head briefly along the cyclepath (above), then bear left along the shared trail across the Common (pond on left)
D. Continue over Cannizaro Road and continue along path on other side

2
A. 100 metres along the train line, where a footbridge (above) crosses the railway, turn right into Alt Grove
B. At the top turn left (St George's Road) then right (Tabor Grove)
C. At the main road cross carefully to the right and head up Malcolm Road

1
A. Head straight over the crossings in front of the station and take path (above) between Currys and WH Smith. Head along path towards the rail lines - it turns right past a car park and down steps. Continue on alongside railway

WIMBLEDON COMMON

Getting there

Wimbledon station is in Zone 3 on the District Line, and also has frequent overland services from Waterloo. Additionally, it's the most westerly station of the Tramlink system.

Opening times

Wimbledon Common doesn't have restricted opening times.

Useful links and other info

Wimbledon Common has interesting management arrangements involving elected conservators. They've got a website (www.wpcc.org.uk), which has some useful information and links, and a bit of historical info on the Common.

One of the main features of the Common is the windmill, now a museum. The route doesn't pass directly by the windmill, but it's useful to note that there are toilets and refreshments there if needed.

Signs and maps

There are some map/information boards around the Common, although these are somewhat sporadic.

You are following part of the Capital Ring on one part of the Common - we have mentioned where there are useful signposts. You will also see yellow and brown stag signs which are markers for the Beverley Brook Walk, although we've not relied on these for navigation.

Refreshments

There's plenty of shopping choice around the station. Where the route first meets the Common (at The Green in 3B) there are a couple of shops including a useful general store just nearby.

Toilets

There are toilets at the station, and also at the Windmill on Wimbledon Common.

Parking

There are plenty of car parks near Wimbledon station. However, although we would encourage you to use public transport, if you are in the car then it might be worth parking up at the Common on Camp Road and picking up the loop from there.

Bike parking

There are bike parking facilities outside the station. If you're just doing the loop, please note there aren't really any bike parking facilities near the corner of Camp Road, although you may find a lamp post to attach your bike to. Consequently we don't recommend cycling to the start of the loop.

Hills and climbs

Total ascent/descent 104 metres

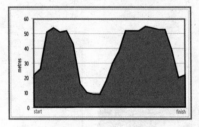

A fantastic 4-mile riverside loop from Barnes to Hammersmith, taking in wooded riverside trails and quaint Chiswick streets

THAMES LOOP 1 – BARNES BRIDGE TO HAMMERSMITH

The first in a set of four tip-top Thames runs

There's something special and 'uniquely London' about running along the banks of the Thames. There's the sense of the natural environment you get from being near the river, and the wide variety of sights and experiences you get along different stretches.

Being Thames-addicts we've included four 'Thames Loops' in the book – two in each of the West and Central sections. These stick closely to the Thames Path, taking you out and back along the banks and over bridges.

If you work in west London this is perfect for a lunchtime run to escape your desk. There's some road running, but mostly riverside tracks and quiet streets where you're untroubled by traffic.

Along the way there are historic pubs, numerous Blue Plaques, lovely houses and good green spaces. Not to mention the spectacular Bazalgette-designed Hammersmith Bridge.

Overall this a great run which gets top marks for being interesting and varied, flat and quiet. What more could you ask for?

KEY FACTS

	4.0 miles / 6.4 kms
	Loop
	Riverside, parks, trails and roads
START FINISH	Barnes Bridge overland station
	Restricted
	Easy. Some wiggly bits following the Thames Path on the north bank
	Hard pavements on the north side, some softer running on south bank SLIPPERY UNDERFOOT FOLLOWING HEAVY RAIN
	Pretty quiet
	As flat as they come – a few short flights of steps up and over bridges
	Mostly traffic-free
	None
P	Near start
	At station
	Nearby (none en route)

THE ROUTE

From Barnes Bridge station you set out along the Thames towards Barnes Village, but head quickly away from the road and along wooded river banks all the way down to the Hammersmith Bridge. Over the other side, you're then heading back towards Barnes on the north bank through riverside Chiswick along the Malls (Upper, Lower and Chiswick) and Terraces, past old pubs and historic houses. Further on the route goes green again as Barnes Bridge comes into view – you take the steps up onto the bridge and cross the Thames back to the station.

THAMES LOOP 1 - BARNES BRIDGE

A. Continue past the pubs and alongside Furnival Gardens
B. At the end, follow path right, but then turn left down the narrow passage (above) past The Dove pub

A. Head along Upper Mall, continuing along the pedestrianised section past the Oldship pub. At the end turn right up towards the Black Lion pub (above)
B. Turn immediately left along Hammersmith Terrace (following a Thames Path sign)
C. Continue on to reach Chiswick Mall – head on alongside the Thames again

A. At the end of Chiswick Mall (above) don't take the path that continues straight on - turn left through a gate to the Thames side again (follow sign 'Pedestrian Route to Dukes Meadow and Chiswick Pier')
B. Continue along the waterfront past the modern Corney Reach Estate and the coastguard station

A. At the end of Corney Reach continue straight on through a gate (above) and bear left into Dukes Meadow
B. Follow the path straight on along the waterfront beside the terraces and sports fields (on right)

A. At the end of the terraces continue on beside the Thames over concrete slipway (above) towards Barnes Bridge and head along path into trees
B. Take steps up and cross Barnes Bridge to arrive back at the station

CHISWICK MALL
CHISWICK EYOT
RIVER
CHURCH STREET
CORNEY REACH
NATURE RESERVE
LONSDALE ROAD
DUKES MEADOW
LONSDALE ROAD
The Bull's Head
CHURCH ROAD
BARNES BRIDGE
THE TERRACE
Barnes Bridge
START FINISH

A. You arrive at the green and gold Hammersmith Bridge (above) – head up onto the bridge and cross the Thames

B. On the other side, take steps down get to the Thames path

C. Turn right and head along the waterfront (Thames on your left) back towards Barnes Bridge

GREAT WEST ROAD
The Dove
Black Lion Oldship
UPPER MALL
UPPER MALL
THAMES
ST PAUL'S SCHOOL
FURNIVAL GARDENS
LOWER MALL
Rutland
The Blue Anchor
HAMMERSMITH BRIDGE

A. Continue along the path through the woods (above)

B. Further on, the school playing fields appear on your right – continue ahead on the riverside path

A. Bear left away from the road to take the path (above) that continues along the riverside

B. Keep heading forward on the path closest to the Thames – ignore path to the right of you

Navigation tips

The north bank looks tricky – and it's true that you've got several sections where you've got to leave the river bank to get around obstructions.

But, as long as you remember to keep the Thames on your left, and make use of the Thames Path signs, you should stay on the route. You're never more than a 50 metres or so from the river, so it's hard to get really lost.

The south bank is a lot more straight forward – just a straight line along the waterfront from Barnes Bridge along to Hammersmith Bridge.

A. Take the steps down from the station

B. Facing the Thames, take the pedestrian crossing to the left of the bridge, then head right along the riverside path (river on left)

C. At the roundabout, continue left along the river following road sign for Hammersmith Bridge (above)

THAMES LOOP 1 - BARNES BRIDGE

Getting there

The route starts and finishes at Barnes Bridge overland station (in Zone 3). Barnes Bridge is on the 'Hounslow Loop' and served by South West Trains. The station is just over 20 minutes from Waterloo on a direct service that also goes through Vauxhall and Clapham Junction.

There are 2-4 trains per hour Monday to Saturday, with a less frequent service on Sundays.

Opening times

The path in front of Corney Reach Estate is often shut at night. If this is the case it is possible to head straight on at the end of Chiswick Mall and find your way around to Dukes Meadow, but it's not our recommend route.

Useful links and other info

The route is partly in the Borough of Richmond (www.richmond.gov.uk) and partly in Hammersmith & Fulham (www.lbhf.gov.uk) - both councils' sites have info on the local area.

There's a wide variety of websites that cover the Thames Path, although the official one is www.nationaltrail.co.uk/thamespath/. It's well worth a look but won't necessarily help you map out a route in detail.

If it's been raining heavily it's worth checking the Environment Agency's website for flooding before you set out - www.environment-agency.gov.uk/subjects/flood/floodwarning/.

Signs and maps

The Thames Path signs are useful, especially on the north bank. But watch out for one at the end of Chiswick Mall - ignore it and follow the route instead.

Refreshments

There aren't any facilities at Barnes Bridge station, although if you head down into Barnes Village there is a good selection of shops.

There's plenty of tempting pubs en route on the north side, but it's probably better to pop back once you've completed the route.

Toilets

None. If you're arriving by train, most South West trains have toilets on them.

Parking

Time-restricted (1 hour) parking in Lonsdale road (free), otherwise pay and display parking on Barnes High Street.

Bike parking

There are some brand new bike racks at the station, at the foot of the steps to platform 2.

Hills and climbs

This route is so flat is doesn't merit a graph really - you're generally between sea level and maybe 2 metres above it.

For the record, the total ascent/descent is approximately 8 metres.

Blue Plaques

There's a whole bunch of Blue Plaques along this route. If you too are a Blue Plaque-spotter then here's a checklist of ones to look out for:

1) Gustav Holst (composer)

2) Edward Johnston (Tube logo designer)

3) Sir Emery Walker (typographer)

4) George Devine (actor & director)

5) Sir Alan Patrick Herbert (humourist, polymath)

6) Eric William Ravilious (artist)

7) Thomas Cobden-Sanderson (artist, bookbinder)

8) The Dove pub (founded 1796) & Doves Press

9) Ninette de Valois (Royal Ballet founder)

A green urban 4.7 miler, looping along the banks of the Thames from Putney Bridge to Hammersmith

THAMES LOOP 2 – PUTNEY BRIDGE TO HAMMERSMITH

More Thames Loop fun

This is a decent loop along the Thames from Putney to Hammersmith Bridge through Fulham and back around the East Bank of the Castelnau/Barnes Peninsula. It's got a really good mix of pavement and track running, is virtually traffic free, and is prefect for a morning run.

There's lots to see along the way – notably Fulham FC's ground on one side and the Harrods Furniture Depository (now posh apartments) on the other. There are also plenty of trendy bits around Hammersmith Bridge (you pass the River Café and the Riverside Studios). The south bank is quite a contrast and feels far more leafy and rural.

During term-time school hours you can listen to sports teachers loudly berating the public school boys (and girls) trying to row up and down the river. Maybe you'll pass some future James Cracknell toiling on the river.

If you're feeling energetic then keep going when you get to Hammersmith Bridge and head down to Barnes following route 13 – we've included a map on page 62 that shows how the two routes link up.

KEY FACTS

🏃	4.7 miles / 7.5 kms
⮁	Loop
🏞	Riverside, formal parks, trails and roads
START FINISH	Putney Bridge Tube station
🕐	Restricted
⬌	Easy. Some wiggly bits following the Thames Path on the north bank
👟	Mostly hard pavements, some softer running on south bank SLIPPERY UNDERFOOT FOLLOWING HEAVY RAIN
🏃🏃	Fairly busy
🔺	Pretty flat
🚗	Pretty much traffic free
🚻	Off route
P	Near station
🚲	At station
☕	At start

THE ROUTE

From Putney Bridge Tube station you head under the bridge itself and into Bishop's Park, then along the waterfront before cutting right away from the river around Fulham FC's ground. Returning to the riverside, you're then heading along to Hammersmith Bridge. You cross the green and gold Hammersmith Bridge, then head back towards Putney along the south bank past the Harrods Furniture Depository building. Further on you head along the Embankment then over Putney Bridge, from where you retrace your steps to the station.

THAMES LOOP 2 - PUTNEY BRIDGE

A. Head up onto Hammersmith Bridge (above) and over the river
B. On the far side drop down to the left and head along the riverside path back towards Putney

A. Continue along the leafy riverside path, past the Harrods Furniture Depository Building (above) and apartments
B. You pass the Steve Fairbairn memorial (bust on right) at the half way point. Shortly after Putney Bridge comes into view
C. Cross a small blue bridge and follow the riverside along the Embankment road (past numerous rowing clubs) up towards Putney Bridge

Navigation tips

Just like route 13, you're never far away from the River Thames. And this one has the added advantage that the Thames is straighter along this section, so you get good early sight of the bridges at either end. Handy for judging how far you've got left to go.

Again, the north bank is trickier than the south, with four wiggles away from the riverside to get around obstacles.

Having said that, as long as you remember to keep heading back to the river wherever possible you'll be fine.

HAMMERSMITH BRIDGE
QUEEN CAROLINE STREET
CRISP ROAD
Chancellors Pub
Chancellors Road
RIVERSIDE STUDIOS
WINSLOW ROAD
7
6
RIVERVIEW GARDENS
KING HENRY'S REACH
RAINVILLE ROAD
5
Crabtree Pub
CRABTREE LANE
HOLYPORT RD
4
MEADOWBANK CL
LONDON WETLAND CENTRE
CROWBERRY CL
WILLSHOT CL
STEVENAGE ROAD
8
FULHAM GROUND
BARN ELMS SCHOOL SPORTS CENTRE
EMBA.
RICHMO

A. Continue up to Putney Bridge (above) and recross the Thames
B. Immediately over the bridge take a set of stone steps (next to bus stop) down to the left
C. Turn left at the bottom and retrace your steps through the tunnel and back to Putney Bridge station

A. Turn right away from the river for the final time along Chancellors Road
B. Turn left along Crisp Road past the Riverside Studios
C. Take the second left (Queen Caroline Street) back to the river again (above) towards Queens Wharf building
D. At the bottom turn right to reach Hammersmith Bridge

A. Continue on the waterfront until you have to turn right again. Head along a wooden-fenced path
B. Turn left again back to the riverside (above) and continue onwards

A. At a red brick building (above) turn right in front of it (not up steps)
B. Head up to a small warehouse – wiggle left then head up a covered path to the main road
C. Turn left along Rainville Road, then follow a Thames Path sign back to the river and continue on. Hammersmith Bridge comes into view

A. The path turns right in front of the football ground – follow it up to the park gate (above)
B. Leave the park and turn left along Stevenage Road past the football ground
C. Immediately after the stadium turn left following a Thames Path sign back to the river. Continue along the waterfront

BISHOP'S AVENUE

BISHOP'S PARK

EMBANKMENT ROAD

A. Take tunnel under Putney Bridge (above) and head through gates to Bishop's Park
B. Turn immediately left up steps to the waterfront path – turn right and head along the river front with park on right

START
FINISH

Putney Bridge

PUTNEY BRIDGE

PUTNEY HIGH ST

A. Take the zebra crossing (above) in front of Putney Bridge Tube station head right along Ranlagh Gardens in front of you
B. Follow the road to the end – turn left towards Willow Bank and Swan Bank Court, and then immediately right again alongside purple and grey building

THAMES LOOP 2 - PUTNEY BRIDGE

Getting there

The route starts and finishes at Putney Bridge Tube station in Zone 2 on the District Line.

Opening times

Bishop's Park is locked at night. It is open by 07.30 and closes at dusk, with an earliest closing time of 19.00 between October and March.

Useful links and other info

The route is mostly in the Borough of Hammersmith & Fulham (www.lbhf.gov.uk). Their website has a set of walking leaflets - useful for devising more routes.

After heavy rain it's worth checking the Environment Agency's website before you set out - www.environment-agency.gov.uk/subjects/flood/floodwarning/.

Signs and maps

You're following the Thames Path for much of this route - this is especially helpful on the north bank.

Refreshments

There's a decent selection of shops around Putney Bridge station at the start/finish of the run, with a more extensive selection on Putney High Street.

Toilets

Near the start of the route there are toilets in Bishop's Park, close to Bishop's Park Road (follow the signs in the Park). On your way along the Embankment back to Putney Bridge there is a 10p toilet machine just after the blue bridge in 8C.

Parking

There is metered car parking in roads around the station, (Ranlagh Gardens and Edenhurst Avenue, amongst others). Typically 80p per half hour, 09.00 - 17.00 Monday to Friday.

Bike parking

Bike parking at the station in Ranlagh Gardens, (under the railway arches just behind the station).

Hills and climbs

Total ascent/descent 21 metres

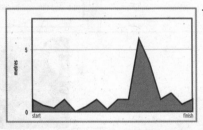

EXTRA ROUTE

For a longer West Thames run just add the two together...

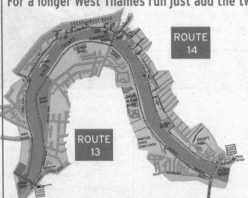

Both of the West Thames Routes (13 and 14) use Hammersmith Bridge to Cross the Thames at one end.

You can therefore put the two together to make a route that heads right over the Castelnau peninsula.

So instead of crossing Hammersmith Bridge, head under it (watch your head) and continue from one route to the other.

You can choose your starting station for what becomes a (roughly) 8.5 mile/13.6km route.

A 5-mile loop around Ealing, taking in the lovely Gunnersbury Park and a couple of West London's other green spaces

WESTERN EXPLORER - SOUTH EALING LOOP

A fast, flat West London loop

This part of West London is blessed with a fair few green spaces - wherever you are there's bound to be one fairly close by to make into a regular haunt. But they tend to be of the smaller variety, and so we've put together an Explorer route linking three of these green spaces with a couple of road sections to make a longer circular route.

Gunnersbury Park is a great place for running. This former home to royalty and the Rothschild family became a public park in the 1920s. There are still echoes of its former grandeur, not least the Mansion house, now home to Gunnersbury Park Museum. A complete circuit of the park is about 2.5 miles - the route we take is just short of a full loop around the fringes of the park taking in some of the historic sights.

The other parks on the route are the pleasant Walpole and Lammas Parks, located next to each other just to the south of Ealing town centre. You also pass Pitshanger Manor Museum and Gallery on the way into the parks. Packed with contemporary art, it's well worth popping back for a visit.

Overall, a great taster for West London running.

KEY FACTS

🏃	5.0 miles / 8.0 kms
🔄	Loop
🏞	Parks and roads
START FINISH	South Ealing Tube station
🕐	Restricted
⟷	Fairly easy
👟	Mostly hard pavements, grass running options alongside paths in the parks
🏃🏃	Quite busy/pretty quiet in places
⛰	Pretty flat
🚗	Three road sections including one long one – fairly quiet roads, several crossings
🚻	At start
P	None
🚲	At station
☕	At station

THE ROUTE

From a start at South Ealing Tube station, cross over the road and through Maytrees Rest Gardens. A few quiet roads later, head into Gunnersbury Park for a near-circuit of the park, taking you past the Potomac Fishing Lake, derelict stables, the Mansion House and round pond. Continue on to almost complete the loop before heading out of the park to begin the long road section. Head over the rail line and up to Ealing Green, from where you head past Pitshanger Manor Museum and into Walpole Park. Continue through Lammas Park, and then a few roads later you complete the loop back at the station.

WESTERN EXPLORER – SOUTH EALING LOOP

9

A. Take the crossing over the road to Ealing Green, then head right up to Pitshanger Manor gates (above)

B. Enter the Manor grounds and head left around the building

C. Continue through gate into Walpole Park – follow path around to left

D. Cross over a small bridge to arrive at a children's play area

10

A. Turn left (children's play area on right) and head straight on along a tree-lined avenue. Bear left at the end and through the gate (above)

11

A. Turn right and cross over into Ellers Road in front, and then left through gate into Lammas Park (above)

B. Take the path to the right. Head all the way through the park sticking to the right hand perimeter (past children's play area on right) to the gates

C. Exit the park. Turn left, then take the first left into Windermere Road

D. Take first right along Trent Avenue, then left at the end. Head up to main road where South Ealing station is just to the right

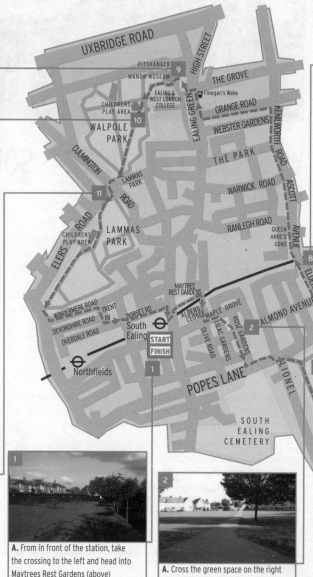

1

A. From in front of the station, take the crossing to the left and head into Maytrees Rest Gardens (above)

B. Head through the gardens and then take the green foot bridge on the right over the railway

C. Head along Olive Road, past the top of Alders Close, and then first left into Maple Grove for 50 metres

2

A. Cross the green space on the right (above) just after Lilac Gardens

B. At the end bear right down Rose Gardens (not down Almond Avenue)

C. Emerge onto the main road (Popes Lane) with cemetery opposite. Turn left along Popes Lane

A. Emerge from the park onto Popes Lane again. Head straight up Elderberry Road opposite (use crossing to the left)
B. Head up and over the rail line and continue straight along until the first mini-roundabout (above)
C. Turn left along Grange Road to the end, and then right at the main road up to the traffic lights

A. Continue along the wooden fence as it runs past the car park and nursery entrance (on right)
B. Head along the access road, then turn left taking the path that runs along edge of park (houses on right)
C. Follow the path around the park heading for the gate where you came in. Halfway along take the only exit path down a brick walled alley (above)

A. Continue past the bottom of the round pond, again keeping left at the end
B. Arrive at a children's play area - turn right uphill along path (above) that runs between the nursery and the bowling green

A. Head past the scaffolded old stables (through bushes on right) to a junction. Continue straight on (not right)
B. Path bears right then up to the low fence (golf area beyond it). Keep to the path that runs closest to the fence heading around to the left past the museum and cafe (on right)

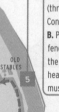

BOWLING GREEN
NURSERIES
ROUND POND
CAFE
MUSEUM
OLD STABLES
CHILDRENS PLAY AREA
PITCH & PUTT GOLF AREA

GUNNERSBURY PARK

KENSINGTON CEMETERY

POTOMAC FISHING LAKE
GOTHIC TOWER

A. Keep heading straight on to the fishing lake entrance gate (above). Circle around beside the railings (lake on left)
B. Continue past the Gothic Tower. At the next junction take the right fork away from the fence
C. Continue on the perimeter path as it runs past the cemetery and then alongside the busy North Circular Road (on right)

A. Gunnersbury Park's gates appear on the opposite side of the road (above). Cross the road and enter the park
B. At the top of the access path (past house on right), turn right to begin circling anticlockwise around the park
C. Head all the way down the side of the park (playing fields on left, houses and then road on right)

WESTERN EXPLORER - SOUTH EALING LOOP

Getting there

The route starts and finishes at South Ealing Tube station. It's in Zone 3 on the Heathrow branch of the Piccadilly Line.

Opening times

Gunnersbury Park, opens at 08.00 each day, Walpole and Lammas Parks at 07.30. They're open until dusk each day, ranging from 17.30 for Walpole and Lammas Parks in January/February through to 22.00 in June/July. The information boards at the entrances display the current opening times (or check the council websites).

Useful links and other info

Gunnerbury Park is in the Borough of Hounslow. The best online place for information on both the park and the museum is www.hounslow.info.

Walpole and Lammas Parks are in Ealing. Their website has information on the parks and includes details of walks in the local area, which could be useful for planning your own running routes - www.ealing.gov.uk/services/leisure/parks_and_open_spaces/.

You'll also find information on Pitshanger Manor Museum on the Ealing site.

Signs and maps

You won't find much in the way of maps and info along the route and none of the parks are very well signposted - but then they are relatively small.

Refreshments

There's a shop at the entrance to South Ealing station, or you can turn right down the main road for wider selection of refreshments.

En route you pass a cafe in Gunnersbury Park, and are close to the main shopping centre in Ealing at the top of Ealing Green.

Toilets

There is a toilet cubicle machine opposite the station (20p). There are toilets in Gunnersbury Park, although not en route. Head for the Museum and follow the signs.

Parking

Car parking is possible in the streets around the station, although it's subject to resident permit holder-only restrictions. Consequently we don't recommend driving to this route.

Bike parking

Bike racks just outside South Ealing Tube station.

Hills and climbs

Total ascent/descent 29 metres

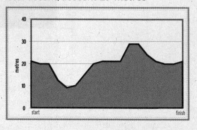

A 5.3 mile loop taking you through one of the Great Cemeteries followed by a section of the Grand Union Canal and wild Wormwood Scrubs

KENSAL GREEN & WORMWOOD SCRUBS

One for really getting away from it all

This route starts by heading through Kensal Green Cemetery, the oldest of London's Magnificent Seven Cemeteries. It's worth investing £1 in the Friends guide (from the gatehouses) and spotting the tombs of the famous and royal as you head along the paths. You also pop through its equally atmospheric Catholic neighbour, St Mary's, at the end of the route. Both cemeteries are still in use, and as with all cemetery routes, please be mindful of those who may be visiting loved ones whilst you're out for a quick run.

Wormwood Scrubs is one of the larger green spaces in West London. It's obviously also famous for the prison, which you can see on the opposite side of the Scrubs to the route. It's a good change of scenery, but a very quiet place for running and we don't recommend doing this route on your own.

Elsewhere, one of the quieter parts of the Grand Union Canal (explored more fully in route 29) makes up most of the rest of the run.

A varied, quiet route with plenty to see along the way.

KEY FACTS

	5.3 miles / 8.5 kms
	Loop
	Cemeteries, canal, roads and heathland
START/FINISH	Kensal Green Tube/overland station
	Restricted
	Easy
	Hard pavements, towpaths and grass paths SLIPPERY/MUDDY AFTER RAIN
	Very quiet
	Undulating
	Some running along fairly busy roads plus a couple of unpedestrianised crossings
	Off route
P	None
	At station
	Off route

THE ROUTE

From Kensal Green station head briefly along Harrow Road before entering Kensal Green cemetery. Loop around to the other gate via the chapel and main avenue and exit the cemetery. A quick road section takes you to the Grand Union Canal, where you head West as far as Old Oak Lane. From here, drop down past the railway depot before entering Wormwood Scrubs. Head all the way along the green path along the top edge of the Scrubs, then up Scrubs Lane. Take the foot gate into St Mary's Cemetery and head through back to Harrow Road, from where you retrace your steps to the station.

KENSAL GREEN & WORMWOOD SCRUBS

Alternative route

Every once in a while we've found the gate into St Mary's Cemetery closed (point 10A).

Kensal Green station is just off Harrow Road, which runs the length of the north side of the cemetery. So, if the gate is closed then continue up Scrubs Lane and turn right along Harrow Road back to the station.

A. Follow the narrow gravel path (above) all the way along and then continue straight on along the tarmac drive past the chapel
B. At the end head left up to the road and retrace your steps to the station

A. After a section with bushes on both right and left, take a left turn past a waste bin through a gap in the bushes onto brick path (above)
B. Head along the path straight up to the road. Turn left and head up Scrubs Lane
C. Pass over the canal on red and blue iron bridge. Cross over to the right hand side at the mini-roundabout and continue up Scrubs Lane

A. Continue past a modern office block (Cumberland House) on left and then alongside a brick wall – take the gate into St Mary's Cemetery on right (above)

A. Head through a gap between 2 clumps of bushes in front of you
B. Through the gap, bear left onto the path that runs alongside the green embankment (above) along the edge of the Scrubs
C. Continue on, heading for the gas tower in the distance. At a wooden fence bear right and continue alongside the bushes (heathland then football pitches on right)

A. Head along road past industrial units then the rail depot on left hand side
B. Cross over to the right before the rail bridges (path on left ends suddenly) and continue under the bridges
C. At the end of the steel fence on the left, cross back over (use the crossing) and double back to go through a gap in the fence (above) into the Scrubs

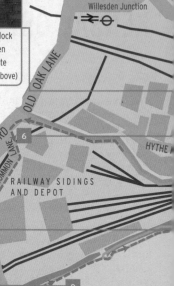

Willesden Junction

OLD OAK LANE

VICTORIA RD

OLD OAK COMMON LANE

HYTHE

RAILWAY SIDINGS AND DEPOT

WELLS HOUSE ROAD

WORMWOO SCRUB

East Acton

WORM SCR PRIS

A. Turn left outside the station towards the traffic lights (above) and the hostel building (with flags in the windows)
B. Cross the main road (use the crossings) to the hostel – turn right and head up Harrow Road (past Masons pub on left)

ALTERNATIVE ROUTE

A. Head left through the cemetery gates (above) and continue straight on past the barrier (not right into St Mary's)
B. Bear left at the first junction, (signpost for 'Cemetery Chapel'), then take next proper left turn (same sign)
C. Arrive at the rear of the chapel – circle around to the front by first turning right then bearing left

A. Head down the steps in front of the chapel and along the main avenue (above) keeping your back to the chapel
B. Continue past a scaffold bar gate, and straight on (ignore a 'way out' sign that points left) along a tarmac path
C. Continue straight on until the other entrance comes into view on the left – leave the cemetery through the gate

HARROW ROAD
HAZEL RD
MORTIMER ROAD
START FINISH
Kensal Green
HARROW ROAD
Masons Arms
ST MARYS ROMAN CATHOLIC CEMETERY
KENSAL GREEN CEMETERY
GRAND UNION CANAL
CANAL
SCRUBS LANE
LADBROOKE GROVE

A. Turn right along Harrow Road up to the junction (church opposite)
B. Turn right down Ladbrooke Grove and up and over the canal bridge
C. Turn right heading down to the towpath and Sainsbury's (above) – bear to the left of the blue tiled building

A. Continue along the canal towpath initially with the cemetery on the opposite side
B. Pass under the Scrubs Lane bridges (above) approx. half way along the canal

A. Pass under a green rail bridge and the new Powerday Wharf (on right), then under a small bridge to arrive at Old Oak Lane bridge (above)
B. Head up to the road (signposted for Willesden Junction and North Acton stations). Turn left up Old Oak Lane, then first left down Old Oak Common Lane

KENSAL GREEN & WORMWOOD SCRUBS

Getting there

The route starts and finishes at Kensal Green Tube/overland station. It's in Zone 2 on the Bakerloo Line. Silverlink Trains on the Euston to Watford Junction line also stop here.

Opening times

The Cemetery opening times are as follows.

Kensal Green Cemetery:

April to September – 09.00 – 18.00
October to March – 09.00 – 17.00

The above times are Monday to Saturday, on Sundays it opens an hour later in the morning.

St Mary's Roman Catholic Cemetery:

April to September – 08.00 – 17.00
October to March – 08.00 – 16.00

The gate from Scrubs Lane into St Mary's is locked half an hour before the main gates.

The above times are Monday to Saturday. On Sundays it opens at 09.15 and bank holidays 10.00 to 17.00.

Useful links and other info

Kensal Green Cemetery has an active Friends society (www.kensalgreen.co.uk/) who run excellent tours on a Sunday afternoon. Their website is jolly good and well worth a visit.

St Mary's RC Cemetery is slightly less famous, but does include a memorial to Belgian World War One soldiers and has a number of famous graves as well.

The Grand Union Canal is managed by British Waterways (www.waterscape.com). It's worth checking their site for towpath closures (www.waterscape.com/boating/stoppages/) before setting out.

Signs and maps

There are a few signs in Kensal Green Cemetery that you're following at the start, but beyond that it's pretty limited.

On the canal there is decent signage with bridges and paths away from the canal well signposted. You need to look out for the sign up onto the road at Old Oak Lane.

Refreshments

There isn't really anything at the station. You pass a Sainsbury's supermarket on the canalside where you can get refreshments.

Toilets

The Sainsbury's on the canalside has toilets if you're shopping there.

Parking

Car parking is awkward around Kensal Green station and we don't recommend driving to this route.

Bike parking

There are bike racks just outside Kensal Green station.

Hills and climbs

Total ascent/descent 44 metres

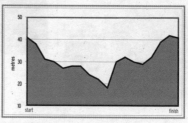

A fantastic, easy-to-navigate 9 mile loop around the edges of Richmond Park taking in all 11 gates

RICHMOND PARK CIRCUIT

So, that's how long a loop of Richmond Park is

When we need a bit of countryside but don't want to trek out of town, we head for Richmond Park.

With plenty of ancient trees, wonderful grasslands and masses of fauna (herons, kestrels and herds of deer) it's a trip back to more rural times. It's the largest and oldest of the Royal Parks with fantastic views around every corner.

It's also a great place for runners – there are paths and trails aplenty criss-crossing the park, and good 'support facilities' (toilets, etc.).

The route we use is a circle of the outer paths for a fairly high mileage run that touches all the park gates. It's an easy-to-navigate introduction to the park.

Highlights on this route include the section alongside Beverley Brook and the quieter paths and trails from Kingston Gate up to Petersham Gate. You don't even see many people along this section – a marked contrast to the easier access areas around, for example, Roehampton Gate.

Overall, a very satisfactory countryside fix.

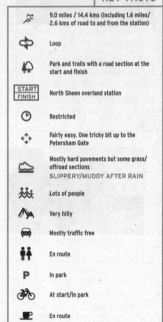

KEY FACTS

	9.0 miles / 14.4 kms (including 1.6 miles/ 2.6 kms of road to and from the station)
	Loop
	Park and trails with a road section at the start and finish
START FINISH	North Sheen overland station
	Restricted
	Fairly easy. One tricky bit up to the Petersham Gate
	Mostly hard pavements but some grass/ offroad sections SLIPPERY/MUDDY AFTER RAIN
	Lots of people
	Very hilly
	Mostly traffic free
	En route
P	In park
	At start/In park
	En route

THE ROUTE

A short road section from North Sheen station takes you to East Sheen Common, and then you're on paths to Richmond Park's Bog Gate. You enter the park and turn left to begin circling clockwise following the main path. You pass Sheen and Roehampton Gates, then follow the course of Beverley Brook for a good off-path section. Rejoining the main path at Robin Hood Gate, you continue south past the busy Kingston Gate. You arrive at Ham Gate and follow a slightly more tricky route off-path up to Petersham Gate, then work around to Richmond Gate on a wooded trail. From Richmond Gate it's a short section back to Bog Gate from where you retrace your steps to the station.

RICHMOND PARK CIRCUIT

A. Take the path away from the station over the footbridge (above). Turn left at the road following sign for East Sheen Common (crossing over the rail line)
B. Head up to the top of Manor Road and take the crossing over the main road

A. Turn left along Sheen Road. As you pass the Courtlands apartment blocks take path to the right away from the road signed 'public footpath' (above)
B. The path runs alongside a brick building and then emerges onto a road

A. Cross over the road (above) with the Richmond Gate on left. Follow the path past a pond (Bishops Gate on left) and further on the Cambrian Gate
B. Continue on up the last climb. Turn left after a fenced enclosure (on left) to reach Bog Gate. Retrace your steps to North Sheen station

A. The path bears right away from the fence and continues, passing several conifer trees (above)
B. Keep straight on towards a red-roofed pub in front to arrive in front of Petersham Gate

13
A. Turn right and bear around to the left up a rough track that heads into the trees (NOT up the big hill towards Pembroke Lodge)
B. The track runs parallel to the perimeter wall. A trail joins from the right - continue left and up a set of steps, then through a gate to arrive at the Richmond Gate

11
A. The trail forks twice more - head straight on each time and then follow the path forward to continue alongside a wire fence (on left)

A. Continue on the main path to arrive at the Ham Gate road (above)
B. Head over the road and take the trail straight on (closest to the pond)
C. After 40 metres the path splits - carry straight on ahead (not left into the field or up steeply to the right)

START
FINISH

North Sheen

MANOR ROAD

SHEEN ROAD

COURTLANDS

EAST SHEEN CEMETERY

EAST SHEEN COMMON

RICHMOND CEMETERY

CAMBRIAN GATE

BISHOP'S GATE

BISHOP'S POND

BOG GATE

HOLLY LODGE PARK OFFICE

SAWYER

RICHMOND GATE

R I C H M O N

PETERSHAM GATE

SIDMOUTH WOOD

PEMBROKE LODGE

WHITE ASH LODGE

PE PON

POND PLANTA

HAM GATE

ISAE PLAN

LADDER

KINGSTON GATE

A. Turn right and head into East Sheen Common past a wooden gate (above)
B. Follow the path to the right of the information board and straight on to reach a gate into Richmond Park (Bog Gate). Head into the park

A. Head forward and take the narrow path to the left of the Nature Reserve Board (above)
B. The path meets the main path - turn left and follow it, heading clockwise around the park

Getting around
Where we refer to the 'main path' we're talking about a 1-2 metres wide compacted gravel and sand path that runs around most of the park.

It's a shared cycle/walking path, so watch out for speeding bikes.

For much of the route you're also following the Tamsin Trail, denoted by small blue arrows. Useful if you need a pointer in the right direction.

SHEEN GATE ADAM'S POND
ROEHAMPTON GATE
ILL
PARK
BEVERLEY BROOK
SPANKERS HILL WOOD
ROBIN HOOD GATE
BROOMFIELD HILL

5
A. You head past the Sheen Gate car park (on left) - follow the path as it crosses a small bridge and over the car park access track around to the Gate
B. Cross the road and continue on the other side taking the right fork
C. You pass Adam's Pond on your right - continue along the main path

6

A. You cross a small footbridge and continue past the lodge to reach the Roehampton Gate
B. Cross the road and continue forward past the car park (above)
C. The path weaves around before crossing over a wooden footbridge
D. The main path continues on - bear left to follow the grass trail that runs beside Beverley Brook

7
A. Continue alongside the brook. At the end of this section the trail curves right and runs parallel to a wall, then rejoins the main path
B. Pass a small car park (on right) to arrive at Robin Hood Gate - cross over the road and continues along the main path on the other side

8
A. The path continues through a wooded section, before beginning to climb steeply past Broomfield Hill
B. Head past the car park on the right. Further on you pass the Ladderstile Gate
C. Continue along the main path on the park perimeter, then over a horse track past a 'Horse track crossing' sign. Carry on to the Kingston Gate

9

A. You cross three small footbridges past the car park to arrive at the road leading to the Kingston Gate. Cross the road and turn right
B. Continue along the main path next to a nature reserve board (above) - not the tarmac one on the roadside

RICHMOND PARK CIRCUIT

Getting there

The route starts and finishes at North Sheen overland station. There are lots of reasons why we start here rather than Richmond station, but ultimately the trip to the park from the station is a whole lot easier (for one thing there's no need to slog past all the shoppers on Richmond high street).

North Sheen is on the Hounslow Loop line, with good services out of Waterloo. It's in Zone 3 (Richmond is in Zone 4).

Opening times

Richmond Park is open from 07.00 each day (07.30 in winter). It closes at dusk – the times vary week by week, but that equates to 21.00 at the height of summer and 16.00 in December and January.

Useful links and other info

This is a Royal Park, and so their website is the first place to head for decent information (www.royalparks.gov.uk), including downloadable maps and parking details.

Signs and maps

There are excellent maps and information boards throughout the park.

The Tamsin Trail markers can be seen along much of the route.

You'll also notice some signs (with a yellow stag on them) along Beverley Brook, which denote the Beverley Brook Walk. These are also to be seen on route 6 through Wimbledon Common.

Refreshments

There aren't any facilities at the station, but there are several options in the park. The main one is the cafe in the car park just after the Roehampton Gate.

Toilets

There are toilets at most of the main gates throughout the park (we've marked some of the principal ones on the map).

Parking

If you're driving to this one head for Richmond Park itself. The Bog Gate doesn't have a car park – head to the Sheen Gate and pick up the route at 5.

Bike parking

There aren't any bike parking facilities at the station, although there are railings to attach a bike to. If you're cycling we'd recommend you head straight up to the park rather than starting at North Sheen station. There are bike parking racks at or near some of the main gates, e.g. Sheen Gate - pick up the route at 5.

Hills and climbs

Total ascent/descent 142 metres

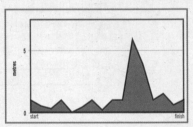

Approximate gate to gate distances

For planning your own routes.

Bog gate to Sheen Gate	0.7 miles/1.1 kms
Sheen Gate to Roehampton Gate	0.5 miles/0.8 kms
Roehampton Gate to Robin Hood Gate	1.3 miles/2.1 kms
Robin Hood Gate to Ladderstile Gate	1.2 miles/1.9 kms
Ladderstile Gate to Kingston Gate	0.7 miles/1.1 kms
Kingston Gate to Ham Gate	0.8 miles/1.3 kms
Ham Gate to Petersham Gate	1.1 miles/1.7 kms
Petersham Gate to Richmond Gate	0.3 miles/0.5 kms
Richmond Gate to Bishop's Gate	0.2 miles/0.3 kms
Bishop's Gate to Cambrian Gate	0.1 miles/0.1 kms
Cambrian Gate to Bog Gate	0.5 miles/0.9 kms

A scenic 10-miler around South West London, taking in some of the best bits of the Thames Path and traversing Richmond Park

BARNES, KEW & RICHMOND CIRCUIT

Sunday mornings taken care of

The final West run combines all that's best about running in this part of London - six miles of unbroken Thames Path plus a couple of miles of trails through Richmond Park. It's a great run if you need a longer route, and are keen on avoiding traffic as much as possible.

Sightseeing-wise there's plenty to look at. There are eight or so bridges, ranging from the very pretty Richmond Bridge - the oldest on the Thames - to the more modern and brutalist Chiswick and Twickenham Bridges.

Elsewhere there are views of Kew Gardens and the King's Observatory in Old Deer Park, and across the river to Syon House and Isleworth.

This is a tough route - although it's pretty much flat around the Thames there's a steep hike up from the river to get to Richmond Hill. It's only 150 linear metres or so, but it's a 1:4 climb.

The views back down to the river from the top are a good excuse to pause and get your breath back before going on to complete rest of this great route.

KEY FACTS

	10 miles / 16 kms
	Loop
	Riverside, parks, trails and roads
START FINISH	Barnes overland station
	Restricted
	Fairly easy
	Mostly hard pavements but with good opportunities for grass running too
	Pretty quiet
	Hilly. One significant climb
	Long stretches are traffic free, but some of road running and roads to cross
	En route
P	At station
	At station
	En route

THE ROUTE

From Barnes station you're heading through the Village to the Thames near Barnes Bridge. A left turn along The Terrace takes you towards Mortlake, and a shimmy right gets you onto the Thames Path. From here it's Thames Path all the way around past Kew Gardens and the Old Deer Park, with good views across the Thames. Shortly after passing under Richmond Bridge you turn away from the river - a steep climb takes you up to and along Richmond Hill into Richmond Park. You loop from Richmond Gate around to Roehampton Gate, and then head along Priory Lane up to Barnes Common. A short section across the Common takes you back to the station.

BARNES, KEW & RICHMOND CIRCUIT

5

A. Continue under Richmond Bridge (above) and along to the end of the waterfront
B. The path turns left and up to Petersham Road – continue straight on into the gardens in front of you (following a 'Capital Ring, Toilets' sign)

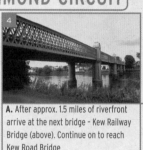

4

A. After approx. 1.5 miles of riverfront arrive at the next bridge – Kew Railway Bridge (above). Continue on to reach Kew Road Bridge
B. Continue along past Kew Gardens. Syon House on the opposite bank marks 3 miles of river completed
C. Further on head past Richmond Lock, and under the Twickenham bridges

6

A. Head through the gardens, then take a flight of steps up to the left (above)
B. Take the pedestrian crossing just to the left over Petersham Road

7

A. Head through the gate to take the steep path across Terrace Field (above). Climb up to Richmond Hill
B. Turn right and head along the road past the Richmond Hill Hotel (on left)

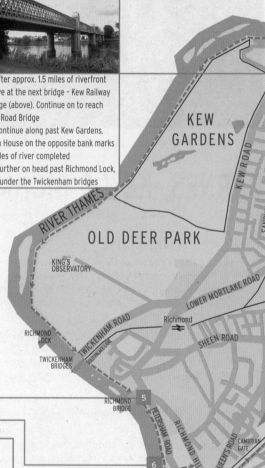

KEW GARDENS

OLD DEER PARK

KING'S OBSERVATORY

RIVER THAMES

KEW ROAD

SANDYCOMBE ROAD

LOWER MORTLAKE ROAD

MANOR ROAD

TWICKENHAM ROAD

Richmond

SHEEN ROAD

RICHMOND LOCK

TWICKENHAM BRIDGES

SOLD PALACE LANE

RICHMOND BRIDGE

PETERSHAM ROAD

RICHMOND HILL

QUEEN'S ROAD

CAMBRIAN GATE

NIGHTINGALE LANE

RICHMOND GATE

Kew Gdns

5
6
7
8
9

8

A. You arrive at the ornate crossing (above) – cross over to the left then turn right and head alongside the brick wall up to Richmond Park
B. Enter the park through the gates

9

A. Inside the park, head forward towards the roundabout, but turn left along the main path (above). This path heads all the way around the park, and is periodically waymarked The Tamsin Trail. Follow the path around the park

A. Continue on the river path passing in front of Ye White Hart pub (above)

B. From here on you are on the Thames Path for just over five miles. In this first section you pass converted warehouses, the Budweiser Brewery and the Ship pub to arrive at the first bridge (Chiswick Bridge). Continue on along the Thames path

A. Follow Barnes High street around to the left and then take zebra crossing over to the river (above)

B. Turn left and head along The Terrace (river on right). Pass under Barnes railway bridge on the footpath and head on alongside Mortlake High Street

A. Barnes station has several exits. Start the run at the phone box next to the station house (above)

B. Head around the front of the station house and along Station Road (with car parking spaces down one side – the other road has yellow lines down both sides)

C. Continue past Vine Road and up to a mini-roundabout. Bear left towards Barnes past the village green (on right)

D. Continue left at the junction following a road sign for Mortlake. Carry on along Barnes High Street

A. Cross carefully at the traffic lights (straight on), then head right to get to the entrance to Barnes Common (above)

B. Enter the Common and head diagonally (following signpost for Barnes station) across on the main path to get back to the station

A. At the Roehampton Gate (above) exit the park and take road to the left (also called Roehampton Gate)

B. Continue on as it bears right then turn right along Bank Road. At the main road (Priory Lane) turn left and head along to traffic lights

Head past several foot gates to arrive at the East Sheen Gate (above) Cross over the road and continue along the perimeter path

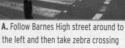

Getting there

The route starts and finishes at Barnes overland station (in Zone 3). It's just under 20 minutes from Waterloo on the Hounslow Loop and Weybridge lines. Both services go through Vauxhall and Clapham Junction.

You could pick up the route fairly easily from the other stations on the map. Usefully, Richmond, East Sheen, Mortlake and Barnes Bridge (not to mention Kew Bridge which is just off the map) have direct service to Barnes if you need a 'get out' part way along the route (Richmond is in Zone 4).

Opening Times

Richmond Park is open from sunrise to sunset each day - see route 17 Richmond Park Circuit for more details.

The Thames Path is periodically flooded, especially in winter. If there's heavy rain check on the Environment Agency's website before you set out - www.environment-agency.gov. uk/subjects/flood/floodwarning/

Useful links and other info

The route is in the Borough of Richmond upon Thames (www.richmond.gov.uk).

Richmond Park is owned and managed by the Royal Parks. Their excellent website - www.royalparks.gov.uk/parks/richmond_park - includes opening times and maps.

Signs and maps

You're following the Thames Path for the riverside bit - and even though it's straightforward it's reassuring to see the signs periodically.

The Thames road bridges all have their names on them too, although they aren't always easy to spot.

In Richmond Park you're following the Tamsin Trail, a fairly well signposted easy navigation route that traces the perimeter of the park.

Refreshments

There's a couple of vending machines at Barnes station, but if you're after something more substantial, then you can stop en route in Barnes Village or around the waterfront in Richmond. There are also facilities just off route in Richmond Park. You can also find water fountains in Richmond Park.

Toilets

In Richmond Park there are toilets at the Richmond and East Sheen gates. Prior to that there is a 10p toilet machine alongside Kew Bridge (head left past the Natural Living Gallery).

Parking

Car parking is available in Station Lane outside Barnes station. You'll be competing with the commuters during the week so it's usually quite busy.

Bike parking

There are good bike parking facilities at the station, although again it's usually pretty busy.

Hills and climbs

Total ascent/descent 80 metres

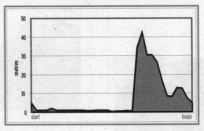

A 3-mile loop around Greenwich, with some pretty tough hillwork. Virtually traffic free

GREENWICH CIRCUIT

Historic Greenwich – including one of the best views in London

This route takes you around all of the key attractions that make Greenwich a favourite with locals and tourists alike. Despite being one of the shorter runs, we think it's challenging, incorporating two testing climbs. If you're starting to put hills into your running then it's a great place to start – the hills are steep but over quickly.

Is the view from the top of Greenwich Park the best in London? Looking down there's a vista from the Dome past Canary Wharf and around to Central London, and with the Queen's House and Naval College in the foreground, it's certainly hard to beat.

Elsewhere, the route takes you through the grounds of the Old Royal Naval College and along the waterfront past Trinity Hospital and Greenwich Power Station. Trinity Hospital dates back to the 1600s, and is the oldest building in Greenwich. It's home to local senior citizens. It's dwarfed by the 20th Century power station next to it – offering a clear view of the clash between old and new scenery that's so typical of London and London running.

KEY FACTS

	3.1 m / 5.0 kms
	Loop
	Historic Greenwich and riverside. Parkland and great views
START FINISH	Cutty Sark DLR station
	Restricted
	Quite tricky
	Mostly tarmac pavements, some cobbled streets, opportunities for grass running in park
	Lots of people
	Hilly
	Mostly traffic free. Some busy roads to cross most with pedestrian crossings
	En route
P	Nearby – not recommended
	Nearby
	Near start and en route

THE ROUTE

From Cutty Sark DLR station head towards the Cutty Sark itself and Greenwich river side. Pass through the Old Royal Naval College grounds and on to Trinity Hospital and Greenwich Power Station. From here turn away from the river up towards Maze Hill, climbing up to Greenwich Park. In the park, it's up again to One Tree Hill and then working around to the Observatory for those panoramic views. Descend to leave the park and head through the grounds of the Maritime Museum, past the Queen's House, and finally back through the College grounds to the Cutty Sark and the DLR station.

GREENWICH CIRCUIT

1
A. Exit the station, turn left and head out of the shopping centre.
B. Head for the Cutty Sark (above). Pass in front of the ship towards Greenwich Pier, then head right towards the Old Royal Naval College
C. Take the gated entrance into the grounds (signposted 'The Dome/River Walk/Toilets')
D. Follow the path all the way along in front of the buildings to the far end

2
A. Head out of the college grounds through red brick gatehouse entrance
B. Turn left down Park Row towards the Trafalgar Tavern (above) and the river, and then along Crane Street (narrow alley down side of the Trafalgar Tavern)

8
A. Take the pedestrian crossing 30 metres to your left
B. Head straight through the gates (above) in front of you and continue forward past the library on your left
C. Turn left after the library and continue through the gates onto the roadside
D. Head right to the Cutty Sark and around the back of the ship to retrace your steps to the station

7
A. Enter the Maritime Museum gardens in front of the James Cook statue
B. Turn right and head along past the museum and the Queen's House. Turn left at the end to pass through the car park and then left again to head around to the Museum entrance
C. Turn your back on the entrance and head through gates onto the road

Tricky bits

Most of the route is straight-forward to navigate. We've rated is as 'quite tricky' however, because we haven't followed the most straight forward route possible in Greenwich Park. Watch out for the bit up to One tree Hill in 4D, and follow the directions in the text not the signs around the park except where mentioned.

3
A. At the end of Crane Street turn left back towards the river and then right along the waterfront
B. Head past Trinity Hospital and the power station. Turn right up the side of the power station (Hoskins Street), crossing Old Woolwich Road and Trafalgar Road
C. Continue up past Maze Hill station (on left)

Maze Hill

4
A. Enter Greenwich Park via the gate on the corner of Park Vista (above)
B. Take first left and head uphill along the perimeter of the park
C. Keep going uphill past one perimeter gate on left
D. At the second gate, turn sharp right and take path immediately next to the one you came up (slightly back on yourself) heading towards One Tree Hill

5
A. Arrive at One Tree Hill (above). Head down the right of the tree following the fenced path
B. At the bottom of the hill arrive at a bench. Cross onto wider tarmac path to the right, continuing on in the same direction
C. After approx. 50 metres turn right and continue on into the wider Bower Avenue, (past formal gardens on your left) to arrive at the Blackheath Gate
D. Turn right and head down Blackheath Avenue (cars parked on either side) towards the Observatory. Pass the Pavilion Tea House and continue along to the General Woolfe Statue

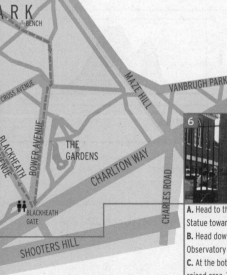

6
A. Head to the left past General Woolfe Statue towards the Observatory
B. Head down the path curving past the Observatory entrance and clock (above)
C. At the bottom arrive at a semi-circular raised area. Take the 2nd path from the one you came down (counting clockwise)
D. Follow path to Maritime Museum gates

GREENWICH CIRCUIT

Getting there

Cutty Sark (for Maritime Greenwich) DLR station is on the Lewisham branch of the DLR network. It's in both Zones 2 & 3. There are frequent services, including weekends.

The route also passes Maze Hill overland station (Zone 3), which is on the line from London Bridge to Dartford (11 minutes from London Bridge). Typically 4 trains per hour during the week at peak and 2 per hour at weekends. If you start at Maze Hill then turn left out of the station and pick up the route at 3D.

Opening Times

This is a daytime only route because of the opening times of the places you pass through. You can do the run between 10.00 and 18.00 in summer and 10.00 and 17.00 in winter.

The Old Royal Naval College grounds are open from 08.00 until 18.00 each day. Greenwich Park is open from 08.00 until dusk daily. The National Maritime Museum and Royal Observatory are open from 10.00 to 18.00 (17.00 in winter) each day.

Useful links and other info

Greenwich Park is a Royal Park – details at www.royalparks.gov.uk/parks/greenwich_park.

The National Maritime Museum and Royal Observatory website is www.nmm.ac.uk. Admission to both is free.

The Old Royal College website is well worth a visit at www.greenwichfoundation.org.uk.

Signs and maps

Like the other Royal Parks, Greenwich Park is pretty well signposted. Especially useful are the maps at the gates with 'You Are Here' stickers.

Refreshments

There are plenty of shops at Cutty Sark station. En route, the Pavilion Tea House in the park is an obvious and pleasant stop. Other refreshments in the park are available during the summer months.

Toilets

The 'best' toilets (free and en route) are at the Blackheath Gate in Greenwich Park. Others also at the Observatory, at the playground when you enter the park and at Greenwich Pier (50p needed).

Parking

Greenwich is not really designed for cars so we strongly recommend using public transport. Car parking is available (but limited) in Park Row and Cutty Sark Gardens (£1+ per hour – run quickly).

Bike parking

Railings around the Cutty Sark Gardens are used, albeit unofficially, for bike parking.

Hills and climbs

Total ascent/descent 73 metres

One Tree Hill

The One tree Hill in this route is not in fact the only one. There's another one in this book, in route 8 (Nunhead Cemetery & Peckham Rye). Here's a few more One Tree Hills...

- One Tree Hill – Honor Oak Park
- One Tree Hill – Greenwich
- One Tree Hill – Brent, London
- One Tree Hill – Auckland, NZ
- One Tree Hill – Adelaide, AUS

A flat 4-miler along the Lee Navigation towpath and around Hackney Marsh playing fields. Takes in the northern fringes of the 2012 Olympic site

HACKNEY MARSH & THE RIVER LEE NAVIGATION

Quiet waterways and open fields

We'd recommend you do this one soon, because it won't be here forever, at least not in this form.

The route skirts the northern end of the Olympic development, including the future locations of the handball arena and media centre. Make this into one of your regular training runs and you'll be able to watch this massive development take shape.

The Lee Navigation is a highlight of the run. It feels very canal-like and peaceful, although it can be quite wet and slippery following heavy rain. Take care if you're out after a downpour.

Beyond the sections of the Lee covered here, it's well worth exploring the waterways for yourself. The Old Ford Locks and Bow Creek are to the south, while further north are Walthamstow Marshes (covered in route 5).

Hackney Marsh is famous for having the most football pitches in Europe. It's also a pretty decent traffic and hill free green space for a run.

Overall this is a typical east London route with green spaces and waterways combined to make a varied and interesting run.

KEY FACTS

	4.2 m / 6.7 kms
	Loop
	Canal towpath, playing fields and woods
START FINISH	Hackney Wick overland station
	Unrestricted
	Easy
	Mostly hard pavements, some off road grass/trail running possible SLIPPERY AFTER HEAVY RAIN
	Very quiet in places
	Flat
	Mostly traffic free - one busy road to cross
	None
P	Nearby - not recommended
	Unofficial
	None

THE ROUTE

The Route starts at Hackney Wick overland station. A short road stretch heads through an industrialised area then quickly down to the Lee Navigation for some gentle towpath following. A mile or so north and you loop around the fringes of Hackney Marsh playing fields, with glimpses of the River Lee through a leafy wood. A short road section heads back to the Canal at Homerton Bridge, where the route rejoins the towpath. You retrace your steps back to the station and home.

A. Carry on along the tarmac path entering the woods. River Lee can be glimpsed alongside (on left)
B. Continue along tarmac path by the waterside (there is an offroad trail that runs parallel on the left – softer underfoot but slippery when wet)
C. The blue and yellow New Spitalfields Market is visible on your left over the river

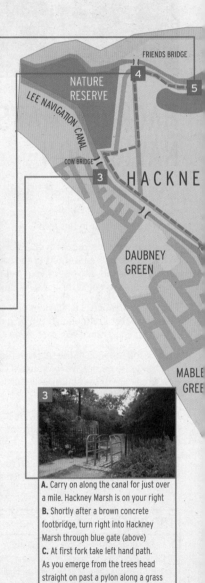

A. You arrive in front of Friends Bridge (red metal bridge) – don't cross it
B. Instead, turn right along the path that runs around the perimeter of the Marsh (above)

The 2012 Olympics

The Olympic development will be mostly to the east of this – to the right of Hackney Wick station in our map. Hackney Marsh isn't being absorbed by the Games, but some of the area near the route (Arena Field on the map) will be transformed into Olympic facilities.

A. Carry on along the canal for just over a mile. Hackney Marsh is on your right
B. Shortly after a brown concrete footbridge, turn right into Hackney Marsh through blue gate (above)
C. At first fork take left hand path. As you emerge from the trees head straight on past a pylon along a grass path, then turn left along tarmac path

6

A. The path and trail join up at White Horse Bridge, which has a sculptural information board in front of it (above)
B. Continue forward in the same direction on the path past the buildings and car park on the right
C. Turn right at the top and head along Homerton Road beside the Marsh

7

A. The road rises to a bridge over the canal – bear right down a path before you cross the bridge
B. Head down to the canalside, arriving in front of the old Lesney Industries factory (above)
C. Turn left under the bridge – retrace your steps along the towpath back to the station

RIVER LEA

ARSH

NEW SPITALFIELDS MARKET

6   WHITE HORSE BRIDGE

CAR PARK

HOMERTON ROAD

WICK FIELD

LEE NAVIGATION

A12

EAST CROSS ROUTE

ARENA FIELD

WATERDEN ROAD

1

A. Exit station (from either platform) by the ramp down to the road. Turn left at the bottom of the ramp
B. Turn left after the closed Lord Napier pub (above) down White Post Lane
C. Head past the industrial units - road bends around to the right
D. Turn left at the end of the road (Lea Tavern pub opposite)

START FINISH

Hackney Wick

1

2

CHAPMAN RD

ROTHBURY ROAD

WALLIS ROAD

WHITE POST LANE

HEPSCOTT RD

Lea Tavern

CARPENTER'S ROAD

2

A. Carry on along the road and over the blue iron bridge (above) that carries the road over the canal
B. Immediately over the bridge, cross the road to the right. Head down onto the canal side (Capital Ring sign directs you down)
C. On the towpath, turn back under the bridge (follow sign for Hackney Marsh)
D. Head along the towpath

HACKNEY MARSH & THE RIVER LEE NAVIGATION

Getting there

The route starts and finishes at Hackney Wick overland station. Hackney Wick is in Zone 2 on the Silverlink North London Line that runs between Stratford/North Woolwich in the east and Richmond in the west (there isn't a Central London terminus). Typically 4 trains per hour in each direction at peak and 2 per hour at weekends.

We recommend using the Journey Planner at www.tfl.gov.uk for getting to and from this route.

Opening Times

The route doesn't pass through any areas affected by specific opening times.

Useful links and other info

The British Waterways site gives details of towpath closures on canals and rivers – it's worth checking their site before you set out www.waterscape.com/boating/stoppages/.

Hackney Wick is in the London Borough of Hackney. Their website is www.hackney.gov.uk. They look after the marsh, including the famous footie pitches.

The London 2012 Olympics website is at www.london2012.org. You can see how things are going and get a map of where the stadia will be built. If you feel inspired, why not volunteer to help out with the running of the Games.

Signs and maps

Hackney Marsh is reasonably well signposted. The sculptural information boards referred to in the text are clearly visible and have interesting historical details on them.

Refreshments

There aren't many shops around here to pick up drinks or food - it's really worth bringing your own.

Toilets

There aren't any facilities on this route.

Parking

You can park fairly easily around the station, especially at weekends. It is very quiet around here so make sure your car is locked and valuables out of sight.

Bike parking

No official bike parking, although there are railings at the bottom of the ramps at Hackney Wick station you can attach a bike to. Again, make sure it's well secured.

Hills and climbs

The total ascent/descent is less than 9 metres with no significant hills en route.

This flat 4-mile run is easy to navigate and packed with fascinating landmarks from the east's industrial past

THE LIMEHOUSE CUT

A history-laden trip along East End waterways...

With paths that follow several of the historic interconnecting waterways of East London, we think this is a fantastic route through areas given a whole new lease of life by sympathetic regeneration.

Early on you're following the Limehouse Cut up to Bow Locks – built so shipping could avoid some of the tricky sections of Bow Creek when heading inland from the Thames.

Further on the two restored waterfront mills make for a picturesque setting. Part of the complex is occupied by film and TV studios – both Big Brother and The Corpse Bride were produced here.

Elsewhere en route there's a Hawksmoor church, reminders of the wonderful Victorian sewer system in the Greenway (which sits on top of the Northern Outfall Sewer) and Abbey Mills Pumping station, and the Channelsea River Path.

There's a choice over where to finish - either West Ham or Stratford. We prefer the slightly longer route through to Stratford, but we've given directions for both.

KEY FACTS

🏃	3.7 miles / 5.9 kms
⟳	Straight line
	Roads, canal towpath, riverside & green paths
START FINISH	Limehouse overland/DLR station / Stratford overland/DLR/Tube station
🕐	Restricted
	Fairly easy
👟	All hard pavements - slippery when wet FLOODING ON SOME SECTIONS AFTER HEAVY RAIN - IMPASSABLE FOLLOWING VERY WET WEATHER LOW BRIDGE HAZARDS ON CANAL
🚶	Pretty quiet
⛰	Pretty flat
🚗	Mostly traffic free - 2 short road sections
🚻	Just off route/at Stratford station
P	None
🚲	Near station
☕	At start, at finish, just off route

THE ROUTE

From the station head along a couple of roads to quickly arrive at the Limehouse Basin. Head left and around the marina, then take the Limehouse Cut up to Bow Locks. Continue on alongside the River Lee to Three Mills, then work around Bow Creek and along the bank of the Channelsea River. Head past the Abbey Mills Pumping Station, and across the Greenway path (on top of the Great Northern Outfall Sewer). West Ham station is accessible from this point. Continue onto Stratford by heading along the Channelsea again - now converted to the Channelsea Path. It's then a short road section up to Stratford station.

THE LIMEHOUSE CUT

Stratford or West Ham....

We do this route from Limehouse to Stratford - but there are some good reasons for nipping down to West Ham station instead. The journey time back to Limehouse is only 5 minutes from West Ham, whereas from Stratford it's closer to 20 minutes and you've got to change. But you do miss out on the final half a mile or so along the Channelsea Path up to Stratford.

If you'd rather stop at West Ham, here's the route:

Starting after point 7C. Turn right immediately after the sewage pump fitting and head along the Greenway. Continue on crossing a road and a bridge. After crossing the bridge, take steps down to your right (a graffiti-ed Capital Ring sign directs you). Turn right at the bottom to get to the road, then follow the road up to West Ham station

A. Carry on along the towpath - there is a mile-long straight section from the Commercial Road bridge to the Blackwall Tunnel Approach Road (A12) bridge
B. Carry on under the A12 along the floating towpath (above), to arrive at Bow Locks on the other side

A. Take metal footbridge (above) over the start of the Limehouse Cut
B. Take steps down to the right, then turn back on yourself under the bridge you just crossed - head away from the Basin along the right hand side of the Cut
C. Continue along the Cut as it bends left - pass under the DLR line again (Hawksmoor church on right here - you see the tops of the spire)

A. Arrive at Limehouse Basin (above) - head left between the water and the arches of the DLR line
B. Cross the wooden bridge - turn right and continue along the side of the Basin working your way around clockwise (past the Limehouse Gallery on your left)

A. Go down the steps from Limehouse station. Turn right and head up to the main road (Railway Tavern pub on left)
B. Turn right, following sign (above) for 'Limehouse Cut & towpath'
C. Take the pedestrian crossing then turn right down Branch Road
D. Once under the DLR bridge, **turn left immediately** down a path in front of Berglen Court Flats (30 metres from top of Branch Road - don't miss it) heading for Limehouse Basin

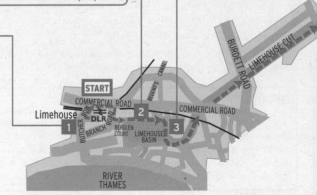

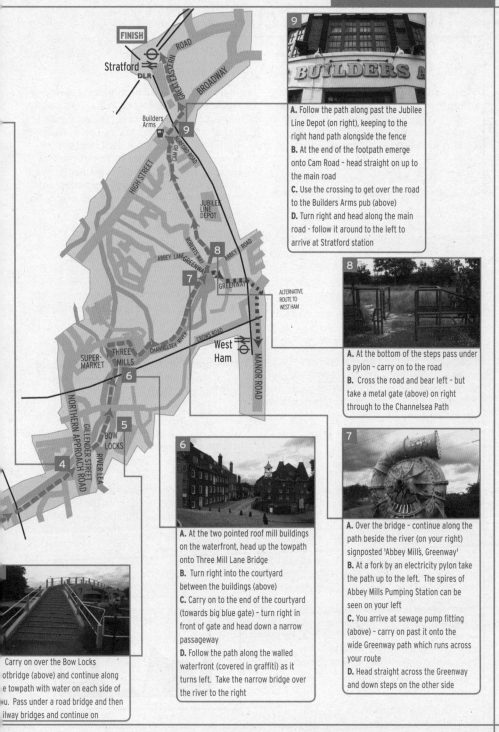

A. Follow the path along past the Jubilee Line Depot (on right), keeping to the right hand path alongside the fence

B. At the end of the footpath emerge onto Cam Road - head straight on up to the main road

C. Use the crossing to get over the road to the Builders Arms pub (above)

D. Turn right and head along the main road - follow it around to the left to arrive at Stratford station

A. At the bottom of the steps pass under a pylon - carry on to the road

B. Cross the road and bear left - but take a metal gate (above) on right through to the Channelsea Path

A. Over the bridge - continue along the path beside the river (on your right) signposted 'Abbey Mills, Greenway'

B. At a fork by an electricity pylon take the path up to the left. The spires of Abbey Mills Pumping Station can be seen on your left

C. You arrive at sewage pump fitting (above) - carry on past it onto the wide Greenway path which runs across your route

D. Head straight across the Greenway and down steps on the other side

A. At the two pointed roof mill buildings on the waterfront, head up the towpath onto Three Mill Lane Bridge

B. Turn right into the courtyard between the buildings (above)

C. Carry on to the end of the courtyard (towards big blue gate) - turn right in front of gate and head down a narrow passageway

D. Follow the path along the walled waterfront (covered in graffiti) as it turns left. Take the narrow bridge over the river to the right

Carry on over the Bow Locks
otbridge (above) and continue along
e towpath with water on each side of
u. Pass under a road bridge and then
ilway bridges and continue on

THE LIMEHOUSE CUT

Getting there

The run starts at Limehouse and then ends at either West Ham or Stratford. All three stations have frequent services but it's worth checking your plans on the Transport for London website (www.tfl.gov.uk).

The route starts at Limehouse DLR/overland station. The overland service is operated by C2C - Limehouse is one stop from Fenchurch Street.

Stratford station is a major transport hub with bus, rail, DLR and Tube links. To get back to Limehouse you need to take the DLR towards Lewisham and change at either West India Quay or Poplar for a service towards Bank or Tower Gateway.

Stratford is also on the Central and Jubilee lines, has frequent trains into Liverpool Street and is a terminus for the Silverlink service.

Finally, you might end up at West Ham - C2C trains towards Fenchurch Street will take you back to Limehouse in 5 minutes, or you can get Hammersmith & City or District Line Tubes into the city.

Limehouse station is in Zone 2, Stratford and West Ham are in Zone 3.

Opening Times

The Greenway is open from 05.30 and closes at 19.00 (October to March) or 21.00 (April to September).

Useful links and other info

British Waterways (www.waterscape.com) look after the Limehouse Cut - see the website for details (worth checking for towpath closures).

The route starts in Tower Hamlets (www.towerhamlets.gov.uk) and passes into Newham (www.newham.gov.uk). Tower Hamlets website has a decent section on its parks and a good selection of walks within its boundaries - useful for planning your own routes.

Signs and maps

There is extensive signage around Limehouse Basin, which will point you in the direction of the Cut if you need help. There are also lots of interesting information boards around the Basin. Along the Cut itself most of the bridges are named - which can be useful for gauging where you are up to. Further on, the Greenway is reasonably well signposted, and the Channelsea Path has signs and information boards too.

Refreshments

There is a kiosk at Limehouse station (peak times only), and shops on the Commercial Road near the start. Once en route there aren't any shops, although there is a Tesco supermarket near Three Mill Lane Bridge. There are shops at both Stratford and West Ham.

Toilets

There aren't any facilities en route, but there are toilets at the Tesco at Three Mills, and at Stratford bus station.

Parking

It's not easy parking around Limehouse, and we don't really recommend driving to this route.

Bike parking

There's no official bike parking at Limehouse. There are railings just up from the station on the Commercial Road, but if you are leaving your bike here make sure it's well secured.

Hills and climbs

Total ascent 15 metres
Total descent 23 metres

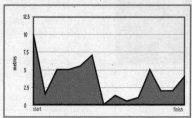

A flat four-mile loop from Canary Wharf, taking in some of the less well known bits of the Isle of Dogs peninsula

CANARY WHARF & THE ISLE OF DOGS

Going to the Dogs (and back again)

Canary Wharf is an interesting, if slightly shocking, change of scenery from much of the rest of east London. It feels big and very modern – and it's economic basis gives it a markedly different feel to the old industrial areas which typify many of the routes we've included in this section.

Given all the financial institutions that have made their homes here, you'll usually find a selection of accountants, bankers and lawyers out for a jog along the Thames Path section of this route.

We've supplemented this well-worn route with some lesser known paths through the middle of the Isle of Dogs, taking in Millwall Park, Mudchute Farm and the docks. It's a little further than turning back at the end of the river front, but it makes for a more interesting run. It's worth noting that it's pretty quiet up through the park – so you might want to run with a friend.

This route doesn't start directly from a station. The DLR is rather buried in the shopping centre – but it's only a short stroll to Cabot Square (follow the centre signs). Use your discretion, especially on the way back. If you've arrived by Tube you can stop running at the Canary Wharf Tube Plaza.

KEY FACTS

	4.3 miles / 6.9 kms
	Loop
	Riverscape, docklands parkland and roads
START FINISH	Canary Wharf DLR/Tube station (make your way to Cabot Square for the actual start)
	Unrestricted
	Fairly easy. Route wiggles a bit along the Thames and you need to keep your wits about you back through the docks
	All hard pavements
	Quite busy along the river Very quiet coming back up the peninsula
	Flat
	A couple of short road sections and some road crossings
	Near start
P	Near start
	Near start
	Near start

THE ROUTE

From Cabot Square it's a short trip down to the Thames Path just beyond Westferry Circus. Follow the path south along the waterfront (with a couple of road sections) to Island Gardens. Then turn your back on the river and head past Island Gardens DLR station and through Millwall Park and Mudchute Farm. Cross East Ferry Road to arrive at Millwall Outer Dock and then weave around the docks up and past South Quay DLR station. Head over a footbridge and sneak through the building in front up to the Canary Wharf Tube Plaza. A quick trip along South Colonnade brings you back to Cabot Square.

CANARY WHARF & THE ISLE OF DOGS

A. Start in Cabot Square with your back to the big tower blocks – head past the fountain (above), down the steps and along the right-hand side of West India Avenue
B. At Westferry Circus, circle around to the right, following signs for 'Canary Wharf Pier' towards the river

A. Head past the Four Seasons Hotel and down the steps (above) to the Thames
B. Turn left and head along the river (signed for 'Isle of Dogs and Thames Path')
C. Continue along the path over Limehouse Lock bridge and past the McDougall Gardens

A. After the Gardens, you pass a redbrick apartment block (above) – follow the Thames Path sign (left) away from the river (past a school) up to the main road
B. You emerge onto Westferry Road – turn right to continue following the Thames Path

A. Carry on until a Thames Path sign (above) – turn right up Ferguson Close
B. Head under the apartment complex through the gates and turn left along the river again
C. You pass Masthouse Terrace Pier and continue along the water front

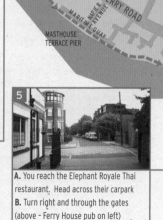

A. You reach the Elephant Royale Thai restaurant. Head across their carpark
B. Turn right and through the gates (above - Ferry House pub on left) Continue straight on along Ferry Lane

Map labels

START
FINISH

1

CABOT SQUARE
WEST INDIA AVENUE

Canary Wharf
DLR

CANADA SQUARE

CHURC PLA

SOUTH COLONNADE

2

CANARY WHARF PIER

LIMEHOUSE LOCK

HERON QUAY

Canary Wharf

Heron Quays
DLR

10

SOUTH DOCK

MARSH WALL

ADMIRALS WAY

South Quay
DLR

9

WEST FERRY ROAD

MILLHARBOUR

MILLWALL INNER DOCK

LONDO ARENA

SIR JOHN MCDOUGAL GARDENS

MUIR FIELD CRES

GLENGAL BRIDGE WEST

ESA

3

ARNHEM PLACE

WESTFERRY PRINTERS

MILLWALL OUTER DOCK

MUDCHUTE

4

FERGUSON CL

MASTHOUSE TERRACE

MARITIME QUAY

MAPLE AVENUE

WEST FERRY ROAD

MASTHOUSE TERRACE PIER

A. Head past the Tube station entrance (on right) and up past the Reuters Clocks (above) to take the steps up to the road
B. Turn left along South Colonade. Cross over in front of Canary Wharf DLR, continue on - turn first right back into Cabot Square

A. You arrive at Marsh Wall road. Using steps to the right, cross over the road and then turn left to pass in front of South Quay Plaza and the DLR station
B. Turn right up Admirals Way (Hilton Hotel on corner) then left at the dockside
C. Cross over the footbridge (above) - head straight through the building in front of you and up across the road to the plaza

A. At the bottom of the steps cross the road and head straight on under the DLR line. Take the steps directly in front of you up to Millwall Outer Dock
B. Turn right and take the path along the dockside following signs for 'South Quay'
C. Arrive at El Faro restaurant - head around it to the left, then left over Glengall Bridge West
D. Head forward past the metal gate and then turn right into Muirfield Crescent and head along the dockside (above)

A. Head straight on along the pedestrian/cycle path into the park
B. Follow the path through the park, initially alongside an old viaduct. When this ends continue following the cycle path
C. The path meets a wall - turn left up a ramp as if you are exiting the park
D. Turn right at the top through the turnstile (above) into Mudchute Farm - take a concrete path that curves up left and carry on to the end of the park along the left hand side. At the end descend left to the road via metal covered steps

A. Ignore a sign for 'Riverside Walkway' and continue on following a sign for 'Greenwich Foot Tunnel' up Saunders Ness Road
B. You arrive at the corner of Island Gardens Park (on right) turn left and head along Douglas Walk. Cross over to Island Gardens DLR station
C. Head right down the side of the station following signs for Mudchute Park & Farm

Alternative start and finish points

We've started this from Cabot Square to avoid confusion and also running through the shopping centre.

But the route passes both Canary Wharf Tube station and DLR station entrances on the way back to Cabot Square. So, if you're returning to one of these, curtail your run at an appropriate point.

CANARY WHARF & THE ISLE OF DOGS

Getting there

You need to get yourself to Canary Wharf, which is on the DLR and also the Jubilee Line in Zone 2.

The route starts and finishes in Cabot Square, which is just outside the Shopping Centre that the DLR sits in. From either station follow the signs for 1 Canada Square (the Canary Wharf building) and/or Cabot Square.

Opening Times

There aren't any restrictions along the route, although the Shopping Centre isn't open 24 hours a day.

Signs and maps

There are plenty of signs around the Canary Wharf area, so it's hard to get very lost. Once you're on the riverside you're following the Thames Path signs.

Mudchute Park & Farm has some map/info boards around.

Refreshments

There are as many shops as you could ever need (probably more) in the Canary Wharf shopping centre. Otherwise you pass a handy little general store on Westferry Road.

Toilets

There are toilets in the shopping centre.

Parking

We don't really recommend driving to this route. There is plenty of parking around Canary Wharf, although it's all paid for and you're not likely to get much change from a fiver.

Bike parking

There are bike parking facilities around Cabot Square. Try to use the official facilities and avoid using railings as you may find your bike has been removed when you return.

Hills and climbs

Given the proximity to the river, you're bouncing around between sea level and the dizzy heights of about 3 metres. For the record, we reckon you've got less than 10 metres of up and down in the whole of the route.

A scenic 7-miler through the City of London Cemetery and around Wanstead Flats and Park. A varied longer run

LONDON CEMETERY & WANSTEAD PARK

Graveyards, parklands, ponds and riverside - the jewel of the east

We think this is one of the best routes in the east - fantastic for a scenic Sunday run.

The City of London cemetery is a beautifully maintained resting place. It's also got two entrance gates, so you can loop around the south of the cemetery. Given it's very much in use and well maintained by the City authority, it hasn't got the faded grandeur of the best of the Magnificent Seven, but it's well worth heading through.

Wanstead Park is somewhere down the usual lists of places to visit, but it's a real treasure. Part of the former grounds of Wanstead House, the Ponds and The Temple are amongst the reminders of its former glory. It's a lovely, tranquil place - you rarely even encounter other runners there.

And in between you've got Alders Brook, the River Roding and the big green Wanstead Flats. Any two of these individually would be fine for a run, but altogether this is part of what London running is about - a run in the city with a great away from it all feel.

KEY FACTS

	6.6 miles / 10.6 kms
	Loop
	Roads, cemetery, trails, riverside and parks
START FINISH	Manor Park overland station
	Restricted
	Very difficult. Some sections require you to set off without good sight of the point you are aiming for
	Some hard pavements, but mostly off road trail running along uneven surfaces **VERY WET IN WINTER**
	Very quiet
	Undulating
	Mostly traffic free - but several road crossings
	En route (near start)
P	Neat station
	At station
	At station

THE ROUTE

From Manor Park station head along the roads past the bottom corner of Wanstead Flats to the City of London Cemetery. Head through the Cemetery around to the South Gate and then trace the perimeter of the cemetery along Alders Brook and further on the River Roding. Enter Wanstead Park and circle the Ornamental Waters. Head past the Temple and then the Heronry and Shoulder of Mutton Ponds. Exit the park and work your way to the western end of Wanstead Flats. The route works anti-clockwise through the Flats and back to Forest Drive and the station.

LONDON CEMETERY & WANSTEAD PARK

8

A. Continue straight on in front of the Temple along a tree-line avenue to arrive at a pond – head through gate in front
B. Continue straight on beside the pond taking the right-hand path where it splits (above). Continue on past a round pond into a wooded section
C. Head on up to the road taking the right hand path near the fence line

7

A. Carry on around the ponds until you arrive at a large pine tree (above) and open area with benches
B. Keep on along the path but take the first right, then the next right. Continue on to reach the Temple buildings

GOLF COURSE

SHOULDER OF MUTTON POND

WANSTEAD FLATS

9

A. At the main road take the pedestrian crossing on left and then head right and left into Blake Hall Crescent
B. Don't follow the Crescent - continue on along Belgrave Road
C. Take a right turn along a 'hidden' path (above) just before Windsor Road
D. Take first left down a rough path that runs along the backs of the houses (playing fields on your right)

10

A. You arrive at a gate (above) – head through it and straight over the road
B. The path is indistinct but head straight in front of you into the Flats. Aim straight ahead, keeping the yellow road chevrons directly behind you
C. Head for a white metal gate that comes into view ahead
D. Pass through the gate and cross over the road into the car park

11

A. Head for the information board (above) - take the path that runs beyond it towards the football pitches
B. You arrive at the pitches - make your way forward and right between the pitches to the far right hand corner, heading for a pub that eventually comes into view (if it's a match day you can turn right here and then left along Capel Road to avoid the football)

12

A. You arrive at the Golden Fleece pub (above) continue along the path that runs parallel to the road (on right)
B. Arrive at the corner of Capel Road and Forest Drive, turn right and retrace your steps to the station

6

A. On the other side of the bridge turn left along a path and over a gated bridge (above) into Wanstead Park
B. Turn immediately right, heading along path parallel to the river (on right)
C. You arrive at a fishing pond - head around the top of it, then left to follow the path alongside the pond (on your left)
D. Continue on beside ponds circling them for approximately 1 mile

5

A. Continue on through a metal gate (above) past an Epping Forest sign on left, then take a right fork and continue along next to the river
B. At the end of the river bank section the path heads up to the left. Turn right at top briefly along a tarmac path
C. At a junction, head straight on (directly under the overhead power cables)
D. Keep on the grass path following the lines of the power cables to arrive at a tarmac road. Turn right and continue on over a bridge

4

A. The allotments wire fence (on right) ends. Continue on for 30 metres then take the next right hand path in front of a set of oak trees. You should find yourself on a path which runs under a pylon (above)
B. Follow the path under the pylon and the along the river bank (river on right)

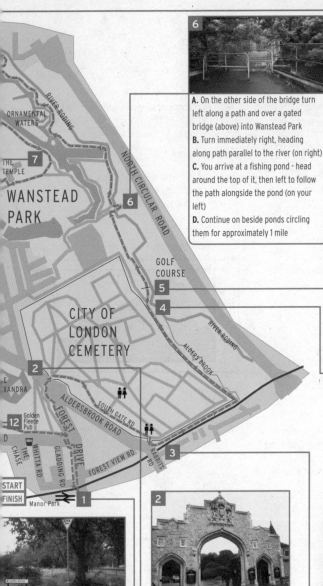

Map labels:
- RIVER RODING
- ORNAMENTAL WATERS
- THE TEMPLE
- WANSTEAD PARK
- NORTH CIRCULAR ROAD
- GOLF COURSE
- CITY OF LONDON CEMETERY
- ALDERS BROOK
- RIVER RODING
- E XANDRA
- Golden Fleece Pub 12
- FOREST DRIVE
- ALDERSBROOK ROAD
- SOUTH GATE RD
- THE CHASE
- WHITTA RD
- GLADDING RD
- FOREST VIEW RD
- RABBITS RD
- D
- START FINISH
- Manor Park
- 7, 6, 5, 4, 2, 3, 1

1

...xit the station, turn left and head up main road (Forest Drive). Ignore the ...en spaces on either side and cross ...r the top of Capel Drive (above) ...continue up the road to the mini-...ndabout at the top of the road

2

A. Cross over to the Gates (above) and enter the Cemetery
B. Turn immediately right along South Gate Road
C. Head right at the first fork, and continue straight across the roundabout
D. Finally turn right down to the other gate to exit the cemetery

3

A. Through the gate turn immediately left and take a narrow path (above)
B. Follow the path as it turns left, continuing to run along the cemetery railings (railway line on right)
C. Turn left again where the rail lines continue on (foot tunnel on right). Continue alongside the cemetery railing with the golf course, Alders Brook and allotments on your right

LONDON CEMETERY & WANSTEAD PARK

Getting there

The route starts and finishes at Manor Park overland station. Manor Park is a Zone 3/4 station on the line that heads out of Liverpool Street to Shenfield. Travel time from Liverpool Street is around 12 minutes.

There are usually 6 trains an hour at peak times and 4 on a Sunday.

Opening Times

Opening times for The City of London Cemetery are:

Summer: 09.00 to 17.00 pm daily (19.00 Monday to Friday)

Winter: 09.00 to 17.00 daily

Useful links and other info

The City of London (www.cityoflondon.gov.uk) owns the Cemetery, along with Wanstead Flats and Wanstead Park. The Flats and Park are part of Epping Forest.

Signs and maps

The City of London Cemetery is well signed and straight forward. Wanstead Park and Flats aren't terribly well signposted although you will find some information boards and maps around.

Refreshments

There is a kiosk at Manor Park station and a corner shop just outside. After that it's very limited.

Toilets

There are toilets in the Cemetery at both sets of gates and also up from the roundabout you cross on the South Gate Road.

Parking

There is metered parking in Manor Park Road down the side of the station (£1.20 for two hours, Monday to Saturday).

Bike parking

There are bike parking facilities at Manor Park station (both inside and on the pavement just in front of the station).

Hills and climbs

Total ascent/descent 34 metres

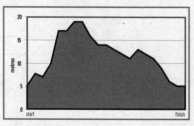

A flat and attractive 8-mile loop of Victoria Park, Regent's Canal and Mile End Park

VICTORIA PARK TO LIMEHOUSE BASIN

Stately splendour and modern urban parkland

Victoria Park was laid out in the 1840's in response to calls from social reformers for the East End working classes to have access to fresh air and an open space. It remains a decent green space – not spectacular but a lovely place for running. The fantastic tree-lined carriage drives are great, especially in hot weather. Its popularity with runners is evidenced by the deep grooves worn into the grass alongside the carriage drives – our near complete loop of the park equates to around 2 miles of the route.

The other main part of the run is made up of two canals: the Hertford Union (albeit only a short stretch) and then the Regent's Canal (all the way down to Limehouse). Both are well looked after and genuinely pleasant places to run. At the bottom of Regent's Canal you loop around Limehouse Basin, adding about half a mile onto the distance.

Ultra-modern Mile End Park is a complete contrast to the stately splendour of its older neighbour. On the way back from Limehouse Basin the route nips over the Green Bridge that rises over Mile End Road and climbs up for a view of the park from New Globe Tavern Gardens Hill.

KEY FACTS

🏃	7.7 miles / 12.3 kms
🔄	loop
🌳	Traditional and modern park and canal towpaths
START FINISH	Bethnal Green Tube station
🕐	Limited opening times
✛	Fairly easy
👟	Hard pavements but with good opportunities for grass running LOW BRIDGE HAZARDS ON CANAL
🏃🏃	Quite busy
⛰	Undulating
🚗	A short quiet road section at the start/end and some road crossings
🚻	Near start
P	None
🚲	Near start
	Near start

THE ROUTE

From Bethnal Green Tube station, head into Museum Gardens and towards Victoria Park. Enter via Bonner Bridge gate and circle clockwise around the perimeter of the park. Having nearly completed a loop, drop down onto the Hertford Union Canal and follow this along to join up with the Regent's Canal. You take this all the way down to Limehouse, complete a circuit of the Basin and head back along the towpath. Turn into Mile End Park and cross over the Green Bridge, before continuing further back up the Regent's Canal. Re-enter Victoria Park through the Arcade Gate and head back to Bonner Bridge, from where you retrace your steps to the station.

VICTORIA PARK TO LIMEHOUSE BASIN

A. Continue to circle clockwise around the park along the carriage drive (above)
B. Pass through two sets of gates and continue along the drive as it bears left

A. Arrive at the Bonner Gates (above). Take the crossing on the right and enter Victoria Park
B. Cross the bridge (canal beneath you) and then turn left through blue gates along the park carriage drive

A. Turn right at the top of Victoria Park Square (past the church on corner)
B. Head along Old Ford Road, then take the first zebra crossing (above)
C. Take the first left into Approach Road (signposted for Victoria Park and London Chest Hospital)

A. Leave Bethnal Green Tube by the 'Cambridge Heath Road (east side)' exit
B. At the top of the steps head right and immediately enter Museum Gardens through the gates (above)
C. Take the path right and circle around the park to the opposite corner - exit onto Victoria Park Square and head left

Map labels: ST AGNES' GATE, GO GA, BISHOP'S WAY, BON GA, Cambridge Heath, CAMBRIDGE HEATH ROAD, Approach Tavern, APPROACH ROAD, R, 4, 3, 2, OLD FORD, ROMA, SUGAR LOAF WALK, VICTORIA PARK SQ, MUSEUM GDNS, 1, Bethnal Green, START FINISH

A. Immediately after the lock take the first gate on the right into Victoria Park (Arcade Gate - above)
B. Turn left and follow the carriage drive around the bottom of the lake. Pass through a set of gates - turn left and back through the Bonner Gates where you entered the park
C. Retrace your steps to Bethnal Green Tube station

A. At the bridge where you joined the Regent's Canal (above) continue over - DON'T turn back down the Hertford Union Canal
B. Instead, carry on along the Regent's Canal up past Old Ford Lock

Navigation tip

Most of the bridges and all the locks have British Waterways name plates on them. Look out for them, especially Johnson's Lock - you need to spot this so you know where to turn into Mile End Park.

A. Bear right, head up the hill and over the Green Bridge. Down the other side take the wide grass steps on right up to the top of Globe Tavern Gardens Hill
B. Carefully take the rough path in front back towards the canal. Head past the sculptures (above), and turn left to rejoin the canal and continue along the towpath

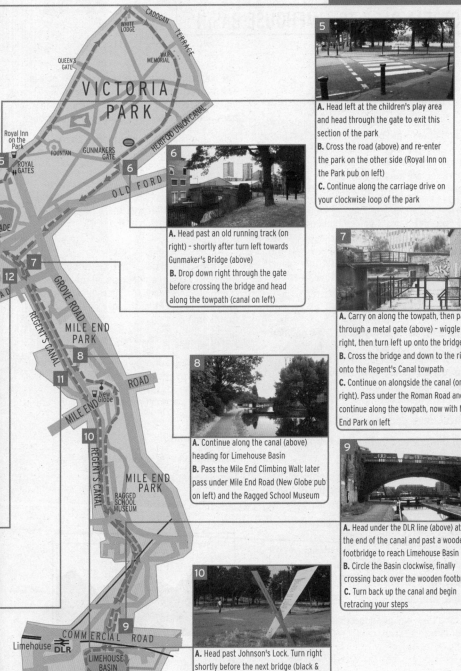

5

A. Head left at the children's play area and head through the gate to exit this section of the park

B. Cross the road (above) and re-enter the park on the other side (Royal Inn on the Park pub on left)

C. Continue along the carriage drive on your clockwise loop of the park

6

A. Head past an old running track (on right) - shortly after turn left towards Gunmaker's Bridge (above)

B. Drop down right through the gate before crossing the bridge and head along the towpath (canal on left)

7

A. Carry on along the towpath, then pass through a metal gate (above) - wiggle right, then turn left up onto the bridge

B. Cross the bridge and down to the right onto the Regent's Canal towpath

C. Continue on alongside the canal (on right). Pass under the Roman Road and continue along the towpath, now with Mile End Park on left

8

A. Continue along the canal (above) heading for Limehouse Basin

B. Pass the Mile End Climbing Wall; later pass under Mile End Road (New Globe pub on left) and the Ragged School Museum

9

A. Head under the DLR line (above) at the end of the canal and past a wooden footbridge to reach Limehouse Basin

B. Circle the Basin clockwise, finally crossing back over the wooden footbridge

C. Turn back up the canal and begin retracing your steps

10

A. Head past Johnson's Lock. Turn right shortly before the next bridge (black & white railings on the canal) to enter Mile End Park heading past the sign (above)

VICTORIA PARK TO LIMEHOUSE BASIN

Getting there

Bethnal Green is on the Central Line (Zone 2).

There are lots of transport links around here - Cambridge Heath overland station is slightly closer to Victoria Park than Bethnal Green but the connections aren't as good and the roads in between are a bit busier. But it's a good alternative if it's more convenient to get to.

Down at Limehouse you can easily pick up DLR and overland trains if you've had enough by then (follow the signs). Further on as you cross the Green Bridge in Mile End Park, you're a stones throw away from Mile End Tube (which is only one stop away from Bethnal Green on the Central Line).

Opening Times

Victoria Park is closed at night. The opening times vary throughout the year but it's generally open from 08.00 each day until dusk. It's worth ringing if you're planning a late afternoon run (0207 364 5000 (the times aren't on the website)).

Useful links and other info

Both Mile End and Victoria Parks are looked after by Tower Hamlets.

Their website (www.towerhamlets.gov.uk) has got a decent section on walks in the Borough, some of which could be good running routes.

The Canals are looked after by British Waterways (www.waterscape.com). The canals are occasionally closed for maintenance - it's worth checking the site before you set out www.waterscape.com/boating/stoppages/.

Signs and maps

Victoria Park has good map/info boards at most entrances, with useful 'You Are Here' blobs on them.

The canal bridges and locks are mostly named. This is important for the route directions as you need to identify Johnson's Lock on the way back along the Regent's Canal from Limehouse.

Limehouse Basin has information boards dotted around it.

Refreshments

There are plenty of little shops near Bethnal Green station. After that there isn't much, so it's worth stocking up at the start.

Toilets

There aren't any toilets at the station. En route there is a 20p toilet machine on the roadside at the Royal Gates (at 5A). There are other toilets in Victoria Park (near the lake), follow signs to find them.

Parking

Parking is difficult. You can park in Victoria Square Gardens (just behind Museum Gardens) at the weekends (permit holders only during the week). We don't recommend driving to this route.

Bike parking

There are bike racks outside the station.

Hills and climbs

Total ascent/descent 29 metres

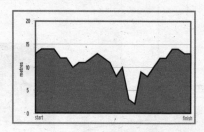

A lunchtime 3-mile dash around one of London's great parks and along the Regent's Canal, with an optional 1.3 mile extension to take in the views from Primrose Hill

REGENT'S PARK & PRIMROSE HILL

Regency grandeur and top views

Regent's Park was designed for the Prince Regent (later George IV) by John Nash in the early 1800s, and was originally intended as an upmarket housing estate for the Prince and his friends. The plan didn't quite materialise - only eight of the villas were built - and the park was subsequently opened to the public in the 1840's.

OK, so Regent's Park is hardly a well-kept secret and we're not telling you anything you didn't know already. You can probably even find your own way easily enough.

But our route does give you a decent run taking in some of the best of the park and using the super-quiet Regent's Canal for a bit of variation. It feels as well-away from Central London as can be and is a real break from the city.

And if you want a little more then we've included an extension section, nipping over the road and taking in Primrose Hill. If you've got the time and fancy a bit of a climb, then it's worth doing at least once - the views over central London and beyond are pretty spectacular.

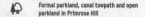

KEY FACTS

🏃	3.2 miles/5.1 km Primrose Hill adds 1.3 miles/2.1 km
⟳	Loop
🌳	Formal parkland, canal towpath and open parkland in Primrose Hill
START FINISH	Great Portland Street Tube station
🕐	Restricted
⟨⟩	Fairly easy
👟	Hard surfaces (paths/towpaths) but grass alongside most paths
👥	Lots of people
⛰	Undulating
🚗	Most of the route is traffic free, but there are a number of main road crossings
🚻	At start and en route
P	None
🚲	Nearby
☕	At start and en route

THE ROUTE

The route starts out at Great Portland Street Tube station. From here you've got to get across the busy A501 Marylebone Road. Once across you're heading into the park and then along the tree lined Broad Walk all the way through the park. You pass London Zoo and then exit the park, heading straight down to the canal (or up Primrose Hill first and then down the canal). After a mile of towpath it's then back up into the park and working your way around past the boating lake and through the lovely southern fringes. You cross back over the Broad Walk and retrace your steps to the station.

REGENT'S PARK & PRIMROSE HILL

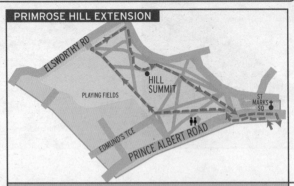

PRIMROSE HILL EXTENSION

ELSWORTHY RD

HILL SUMMIT

PLAYING FIELDS

ST MARKS SQ

EDMUND'S TCE

PRINCE ALBERT ROAD

PRIMROSE HILL EXTENSION

4

3

LONDON ZO

PRINCE ALBERT ROAD

REGENT'S CANAL

OUTER CIRCLE

REGENT

THE HL

Turn left along Prince Albert Road and head past the Zoo entrance

Take crossing over to red phone box – this is a key landmark for getting around the extension – and enter Primrose Hill

From here there are lots of paths you can take to get up to the hill – to get a full 1.3 miles take the path to the left and head past the children's play area. You arrive at a gate. From there, head alongside the playing fields and circle around the outer edges of Primrose Hill before climbing up the back of the summit. Coming this way the views are all laid out in front of you. You then head downhill to towards the red phone box and retrace your steps back to rejoin the main route at the canal bridge

5

5

WINFIELD HOUSE

6

BOAT HOUSE

A. Continue along the towpath until you're approaching Chalbert Street Bridge (above)
B. Turn right before the bridge then double back up the path onto the bridge
C. Cross the canal and continue over the main road to re-enter the park
D. At the first fork head right – continue bearing right around the fenced grounds of Winfield House (on right)

6

A. Head past an ice-cream kiosk on left (above), turning right over two blue wooden bridges
B. You arrive on the south side of the lake. Turn left and head past the boat house (on left) and continue on the path sticking to the shore of the lake

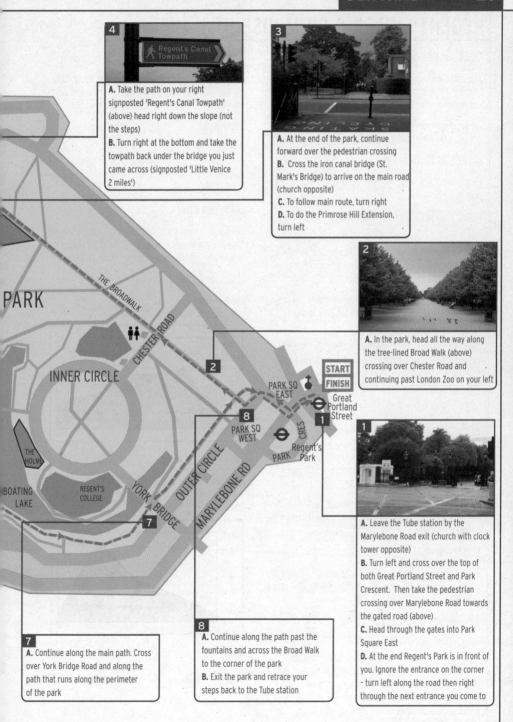

4

Regent's Canal Towpath

A. Take the path on your right signposted 'Regent's Canal Towpath' (above) head right down the slope (not the steps)
B. Turn right at the bottom and take the towpath back under the bridge you just came across (signposted 'Little Venice 2 miles')

3

A. At the end of the park, continue forward over the pedestrian crossing
B. Cross the iron canal bridge (St. Mark's Bridge) to arrive on the main road (church opposite)
C. To follow main route, turn right
D. To do the Primrose Hill Extension, turn left

2

A. In the park, head all the way along the tree-lined Broad Walk (above) crossing over Chester Road and continuing past London Zoo on your left

THE BROADWALK

CHESTER ROAD

PARK

INNER CIRCLE

2

PARK SQ EAST

START FINISH

Great Portland Street

1

THE HOLME

8

PARK SQ WEST

PARK CRES

Regent's Park

BOATING LAKE

REGENT'S COLLEGE

YORK BRIDGE

OUTER CIRCLE

MARYLEBONE RD

7

1

A. Leave the Tube station by the Marylebone Road exit (church with clock tower opposite)
B. Turn left and cross over the top of both Great Portland Street and Park Crescent. Then take the pedestrian crossing over Marylebone Road towards the gated road (above)
C. Head through the gates into Park Square East
D. At the end Regent's Park is in front of you. Ignore the entrance on the corner – turn left along the road then right through the next entrance you come to

7

A. Continue along the main path. Cross over York Bridge Road and along the path that runs along the perimeter of the park

8

A. Continue along the path past the fountains and across the Broad Walk to the corner of the park
B. Exit the park and retrace your steps back to the Tube station

REGENT'S PARK & PRIMROSE HILL

Getting there

The route starts and finishes at Great Portland Street Tube station (Circle, Metropolitan and Hammersmith & City lines). It's in Zone 1.

Regent's Park Tube station is closed for refurbishment until mid-2007.

Opening times

Regent's Park is open from 05.00 to dusk each day.

Useful links and other info

Both Regent's Park and Primrose Hill are owned and managed by the Royal Parks. See their website (www.royalparks.gov.uk) for lots of useful information.

The Royal Park's information centre is located at the junction of Chester Road and Inner Circle.

The Regent's Canal is looked after by British Waterways (www.waterscape.com). The canal towpath is occasionally closed – it's worth checking their site for stoppages.

Signs and maps

There are plenty of official map boards around the park gates, which have 'You Are Here' locations marked on them (although not in Primrose Hill). The paths through the park are mostly unsignposted.

The canal bridges are well marked and named, many signs including further information or historical facts.

Refreshments

There are cafes and shops including a Tesco at Great Portland Street Tube station. There are cafes and kiosks en route.

Other facilities

In the middle of the Park is The Hub, which you can use for changing, showering and secure kit storage. Open from 9.00 each day (closing times vary), £1.50 for a shower and £1 (returnable) for the lockers. Enquiries 020 7935 2458 or thehub@royalparks.gsi.gov.uk

Toilets

There are decent toilets at Great Portland Street Tube – there are also plenty around Regent's Park itself, including en route.

Parking

Because of the traffic in central London we don't recommend driving to this route. There is metered parking on Chester Road if you need it.

Bike parking

None at Great Portland Street Tube station. Some of the park gates have cycle racks and there are cycle racks at the Hub.

Hills and climbs

Main route
Total ascent/descent 18 metres

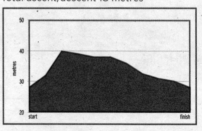

Primrose Hill Extension

Total ascent/descent 35 metres (assuming you follow our route looping around and back over the Hill)

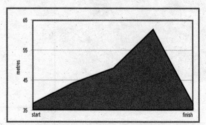

A 4.5 mile loop criss-crossing the Thames to bag the best bits of this part of town – the Tower of London, St Paul's, Tate Modern, the Golden Hinde, Tower Bridge, HMS Belfast and City Hall

THAMES LOOP 3 – TOWER HILL & ST PAUL'S

Sight-seeing at speed – on your marks

This is one of a pair of Thames-side routes in Central London, each of them taking in some of the great sights and guidebook highlights the city has to offer. It's a fun run.

If there is a downside, especially during the summer, it's the number of moving obstacles (i.e. visitors) to contend with. It's worth remembering that whilst you're running everyone else is looking, usually up, so it's up to you to avoid collisions.

The view up to St Paul's as you head along the Millennium Bridge is one of the best in the capital – no wonder it seems to feature on the cover of every other London guidebook.

From a runners point of view it's as traffic-free as they come and also a popular area with others afflicted with the running bug, so you're seldom alone.

Navigationally it's fairly straightforward, although there is a fair bit of wiggling about. We could have made it simpler but then you wouldn't have bagged so many bridges and would have had to miss out on some of the sights. So, no apologies – it's well worth the effort.

KEY FACTS

🏃	4.5 miles /7.2 kms
🔄	Loop
🏞	Riverscape – past some of London's most notable tourist sights
START FINISH	Tower Hill Tube station
🕐	Unrestricted
✥	Fairly easy
👟	All hard surfaces – pavements, including cobbled streets
🏃🏃	Lots of people
⛰	Hilly
🚗	Virtually traffic-free
🚻	Near start
P	None
🚲	None
☕	Near start and en route

THE ROUTE

From Tower Hill Tube station take the underpass to the Tower of London itself. Head down the ticket office plaza, arriving quickly Thames-side. You pass under London Bridge and Cannon Street rail bridge, then over to the south bank via Southwark Bridge. Continuing upstream past the The Globe, you arrive at Tate Modern, it's then back over the river via the Millennium Bridge for a loop of St Paul's. Back to the river, over Blackfriars Bridge and along the south bank again. Passing under Southwark Bridge this time, you head past Vinopolis and the Clink Prison Museum, the Golden Hinde and Southwark Cathedral. Beside the river again, you're then on the home stretch past HMS Belfast and City Hall up to Tower Bridge and the station.

THAMES LOOP 3 - TOWER HILL & ST PAUL'S

A. Take the pedestrian crossing to the left, then turn right alongside the cathedral
B. Take the gate (above) into the cathedral gardens and head past a golden statue of St Paul
C. Continue to circle around the cathedral anti-clockwise to arrive back at the pedestrian crossing. Retrace your steps back towards the Thames (not all the way)

A. In front of Tate Modern, cross the Thames again over the Millennium Footbridge (above)
B. On the far side keep going until you arrive in front of St Paul's

A. Turn right into Fruiterers' Passage before Southwark Bridge
B. Through the passage, turn immed' back left (blind corner) and up the s' via Three Barrels Walk (above). Cross river over Southwark Bridge
C. Over the bridge take the steps dow the right and continue along the Tha again, past the Globe Theatre (on lef

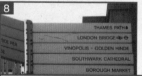

A. Cross back over Queen Victoria Street, then turn right in front of the City of London School (look out for the City's coat of arms on the wall)
B. Head down White Lion Hill and take the second set of steps you come to (above), arriving down on the riverside
C. Head right along Paul's Walk, under the rail bridge and up the steps onto Blackfriars Bridge and across the river

A. Across the bridge, take steps down to the left
B. Head under the rail bridge, past the Founders Arms and then Tate Modern
C. Continue back to Southwark Bridge and follow the sign (above) right, under the bridge towards London Bridge station and Vinopolis

A. Follow the path as it bears right past the Anchor pub
B. Turn left between Vinopolis and Wagamama under the bridge. Continue on past the Clink Prison Museum
C. Follow the road to the Golden Hinde and bear right again away from the river

A. Turn immediately left around the back of Southwark Cathedral
B. Head past the statue (above) and along Montague Close
C. Continue past the Mudlark pub on your right and under London Bridge again

Take care

Please keep your wits about you and look out for pedestrians - especially along 'The Walks' on the north bank - lots of corners for people to suddenly emerge from

. Keep on beside the Thames along the Walks. Continue on underneath London Bridge (above)
. Turn right away from the river at Allhallow's Lane
. Turn left through Steelyard Passage under Cannon Street railway bridge
. Turn left and continue along the river

A. Turn left and head down the plaza towards the Tower Shop and tree (above)
B. Bear right to head for a sign 'Tower Pier and Boats' - pass through gate down Three Quays Walk
C. Turn right and head along the Thames

A. From in front of the Tube station, follow the signs for The Tower of London under Tower Hill underpass (above)
B. On the other side turn right and head up the ramp towards the ticket office plaza

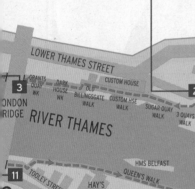

A. Across the river, take steps in the middle of the bridge (above) downwards
B. Turn immediately left and through the gate into the Tower Wharf area (in front of the Tower of London)
C. Head all the way along to the Tower Shop, then retrace your steps up the plaza and back to the Tube station

A. Continue along Tooley Street
B. At the Art Deco St Olaf House (above) turn left back towards the river (path signposted 'Queens Walk')
C. Turn right at the bottom and head along the Thames Path (past Hay's Galleria, HMS Belfast and City Hall

A. Arrive at Tower Bridge. Climb the steps (above) signposted 'Tower Bridge Exhibition'
B. Cross the Thames for the last time

THAMES LOOP 3 - TOWER HILL & ST PAUL'S

Getting there

The route starts and finishes at Tower Hill Tube station (Zone 1, District & Circle Lines). Tower Gateway (DLR) is nearby.

Opening times

There aren't any official opening times along this route.

Useful links and other info

Most decent London guidebooks will give you plenty of information on the area and the sights along the way. There is a Tourist Information Centre at Vinopolis.

For further info on the north bank see www.cityoflondon.gov.uk and for the south bank www.southbanklondon.com.

Signs and maps

For much of the route you're following bits of the Thames Path. It's well signposted where you're close to the Thames which is great, but you're away from it around St Paul's and so will need to follow our route carefully.

Refreshments

There are plenty of fast food places around the Tower of London ticket office plaza. There is also a kiosk outside the Tube station (upper level). The route passes plenty of other shops and food places along the way.

Toilets

The 'best' toilets (free and en route) are at Tower of London ticket office plaza. There are others en route on the embankments, some of which you'll need change (20p or 50p) for.

Parking

Being in Central London, this really isn't a 'drive-to' route, and we can't recommend where to park if you do.

Bike parking

One of the more awkward ones. There isn't any official bike parking at Tower Hill Tube station. There are railings around, but it's not great and so we don't recommend cycling to this route.

Hills and climbs

Total ascent/descent 38 metres

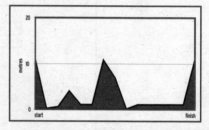

Extra route

You can combine this with route 27 to do a longer (8 mile) run. See page 114 for details.

The last of our four Thames Loops – a pleasant 4-miler taking in the Mother of all Parliaments and the sights of the South Bank

THAMES LOOP 4 – WESTMINSTER & THE SOUTH BANK

More tourist-dodging along the Thames

Thames Loop 4 is a little greener and a little easier to navigate than route 26. The pay off is that there's a bit further to go along busy roads.

From a sightseeing perspective you can't miss the Houses of Parliament and 'Big Ben', – the route circles around both. Big Ben's official name is the Clock Tower, with Big Ben being the name of the main bell within the clock mechanism. Around the world it's perhaps the most recognisable London landmark.

On the South Bank the London Eye is a now familiar feature on the river skyline. It's the largest of its kind and has more than 3.5 million visitors each year. The sheer scale of it is truly amazing the first time you get up close.

It's worth pointing out that again there's lots of human traffic along the way, especially in front of the old County Hall (just after the London Eye, where the Aquarium is) and sometimes around Parliament Square.

But we think that's part of the fun – cruising through the crowds as they're enjoying their day out is a good feeling.

KEY FACTS

🏃	4.0 miles /6.4 kms
🔄	Loop
🌳	Riverscape including tourist highlights, roads and gardens
START FINISH	Embankment Tube station
🕐	Restricted
↔	Easy
👟	Pavements throughout
👫	Lots of people
⛰	Pretty flat
🚗	Some roads, one pedestrianised crossing
🚻	Near station
P	None
🚲	At station
☕	Near station

THE ROUTE

From Embankment Tube station you head straight into and through Embankment Gardens to arrive out onto the Victoria Embankment for a section of determined road running beside the Thames. You cross Blackfriars Bridge over to the South Bank and turn back to head along the river again past the National Theatre, Festival Hall, the London Eye, Dali Universe and London Aquarium. You cross Westminster Bridge and circle the Houses of Parliament before passing through Victoria Tower Gardens. You cross Lambeth Bridge back over the Thames and head along back past The Eye to the Golden Jubilee Footbridge, crossing back to the station.

THAMES LOOP 4 - WESTMINSTER & THE SOUTH BANK

1

A. Leave Embankment Tube station by the Charing Cross exit (not Embankment Pier)
B. Turn immediately right, past the bike racks and take the gate (above) into Embankment Gardens
C. Pass through a second gate and continue straight on through the gardens
D. At the end, exit onto the main road - take crossing over to the river side (Queen Mary in front of you)

8

A. Over the bridge, turn left down the steps and head back along the Embankment (Lambeth Palace on right)
B. Continue under Westminster Bridge again and retrace your steps past London Aquarium and the London Eye
C. Take the first Golden Jubilee Footbridge (above) over the river
D. On the other side head right in front of the Playhouse Theatre, pass under the bridge to emerge back at the Tube station

7

A. At the end of the Houses of Parliament, turn left into Victoria Tower Gardens (statue of Emmeline Pankhurst, above, in front of you)
B. Turn right and follow path diagonally past sculpture (the Burghers of Calais) to the river bank
C. Turn right and head along with the river on your left
D. At the end of the gardens take steps up onto Lambeth Bridge and turn left recrossing the river

6

A. Head over towards the Houses of Parliament (above) and then circle the buildings around to the left through Parliament Square
B. Continue past the rear of Westminster Abbey (over the road on the right)

Charing Cross

EMBANKMENT GDNS

START FINISH

1

CLEOPAT
NEED

Embankm

NORTHUMBERLAND AVENUE

GOLDEN JU

GOLDEN JUBIL

HORSEGUARDS AVENUE

BANQUETING HOUSE

WHITEHALL

VICTORIA EMBANKMENT

LON

Westminster

WESTMINST
BRIDGE

PARLIAMENT

6

SQUARE

HOUSES OF PARLIAMENT

WESTMINSTER ABBEY

RIVER THAMES

VICTORIA TOWER GDNS

7

MILLBANK

LAMBETH BRIDGE

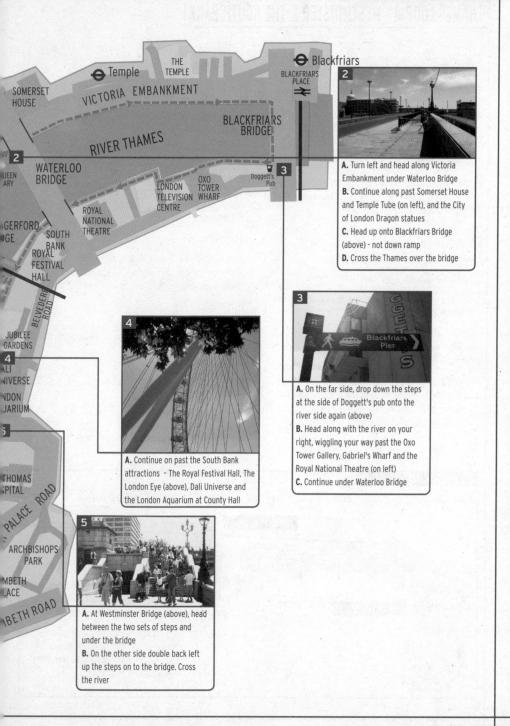

SOMERSET
HOUSE

Temple

THE
TEMPLE

Blackfriars

BLACKFRIARS
PLACE

VICTORIA EMBANKMENT

BLACKFRIARS
BRIDGE

RIVER THAMES

2

WATERLOO
BRIDGE

QUEEN
MARY

Doggett's
Pub

3

LONDON
TELEVISION
CENTRE

OXO
TOWER
WHARF

ROYAL
NATIONAL
THEATRE

HUNGERFORD
BRIDGE

SOUTH
BANK

ROYAL
FESTIVAL
HALL

BELVEDERE
ROAD

JUBILEE
GARDENS

4

DALI
UNIVERSE

LONDON
AQUARIUM

ST THOMAS
HOSPITAL

PALACE ROAD

ARCHBISHOPS
PARK

LAMBETH
PALACE

LAMBETH ROAD

2

A. Turn left and head along Victoria
Embankment under Waterloo Bridge
B. Continue along past Somerset House
and Temple Tube (on left), and the City
of London Dragon statues
C. Head up onto Blackfriars Bridge
(above) - not down ramp
D. Cross the Thames over the bridge

3

A. On the far side, drop down the steps
at the side of Doggett's pub onto the
river side again (above)
B. Head along with the river on your
right, wiggling your way past the Oxo
Tower Gallery, Gabriel's Wharf and the
Royal National Theatre (on left)
C. Continue under Waterloo Bridge

4

A. Continue on past the South Bank
attractions – The Royal Festival Hall, The
London Eye (above), Dali Universe and
the London Aquarium at County Hall

5

A. At Westminster Bridge (above), head
between the two sets of steps and
under the bridge
B. On the other side double back left
up the steps on to the bridge. Cross
the river

Getting there

The route starts and finishes at Embankment Tube station (Zone 1, District & Circle, Bakerloo and Northern Lines). Embankment station is only a stone's throw from Charing Cross, which is a major overland station.

Opening times

Embankment Gardens open at 07.30 each day, and close at dusk each day (varying from 17.00 to 21.00 depending on the time of year).

Victoria Tower Gardens are also shut at night, with similar opening times to Embankment Gardens.

Useful links and other info

The links and further info are similar to those for route 26.

Additionally, the Houses of Parliament website has information on the Palace of Westminster (www.parliament.uk/about/visiting.cfm).

County Hall (www.londoncountyhall.com) has a site that has weblinks to the London Aquarium, London Eye and Dali Universe sites where you can find further details and book tickets.

Signs and maps

You're following the Thames Path for part of this route, although the navigation is fairly simple and doesn't rely heavily on the Thames Path signage.

The South Bank is pretty well signposted too, and so you can check your progress as you go.

Refreshments

There are lots of shops around Embankment Tube station.

Toilets

There are toilets near Embankment Tube station - follow the signs. There aren't any recommended toilets en route.

Parking

We don't recommend driving to this route because parking is tricky around the start.

Bike parking

There is bike parking just outside the Tube station.

Hills and climbs

The total ascent/decent is 22 metres.

EXTRA ROUTE

You can put routes 26 and 27 together for a longer Central Thames run

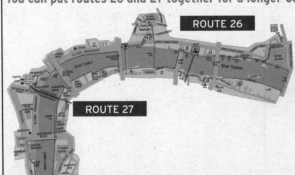

ROUTE 26

ROUTE 27

Routes 26 (Tower Hill & St Paul's) and 27 (Westminster & The South Bank) both cross Blackfriars Bridge.

So, it's possible to join the two at Blackfriars and put together a circuit of around 8 miles/ 13 kms.

It's probably worth doing each route separately first to get a feel for them before you put the whole thing together.

A 4-mile loop from Sloane Square Tube station to Battersea Park, crossing the Thames over the beautiful and much-loved Albert Bridge

SLOANE SQUARE TO BATTERSEA PARK

A slice of Victorian London

Battersea Park is a gem of a green space only a mile or so from the retail delights of Sloane Square. Although there are closer rail stations, this route gets you away from the middle of town quickly and takes you through the historic and attractive back streets of Chelsea.

As you get down to the river you also head down part of Cheyne Walk. There are Blue Plaques on this section for George Eliot and the artist and poet Dante Rossetti. Although there's plenty more on the other side of Cheyne Walk (including King Henry VII) and you can see the houses where Mick Jagger and Keith Richards used to live, we head over the Thames via Albert Bridge.

Dating from the 1870s, it hasn't been the most robust of bridges, needing strengthening over the years. Due for replacement at one point, it was saved by public outcry. It remains a pretty delicate bridge – hence the 2 tonne traffic limit and the instruction to marching soldiers to break their step to avoid vibrations. As for runners, unless you're en masse and of the larger variety, it should be alright.

KEY FACTS

🏃	4.4 miles / 7.0 kms
⇄	Loop
🌳	Roads, riverside and park
START FINISH	Sloane Square Tube station
⏱	Restricted
↔	Fairly easy
👟	Mixed – tarmac pavements throughout but with grass options in the park
👥	Lots of people
⛰	Flat
🚗	The road sections are pretty quiet considering this is Central London. Main crossings are pedestrianised
🚻	Nearby
P	Not recommended
🚲	At station
☕	Near start and en route

THE ROUTE

From Sloane Square Tube station you head down the red-brick Sloane Gardens, crossing Lower Sloane Street at the bottom. You're then around the back of Chelsea Hospital along Turk's Row, Franklin's Row and St. Leonard's Terrace past Royal Avenue. Carrying on, you turn into Flood Street and down the celebrated Cheyne Walk, then across Chelsea Embankment and over Albert Bridge. A loop along the riverside and around Battersea Park's Carriage Drives brings you back to Albert Bridge, from where you retrace your steps to the station.

SLOANE SQUARE TO BATTERSEA PARK

1

A. From in front of the Tube station cross over the road to the Hugo Boss store opposite. Turn left down Sloane Gardens (above) and follow it to the end
B. Take the zebra crossing to your left over Lower Sloane Square
C. Turn right down Turk's Row (Rose & Crown pub on corner)

2

A. At the end of Turk's Row turn right into Franklin's Row, then left along St Leonard's Terrace (green space on left)
B. Continue along Tedworth Square and then Redesdale Street
C. Turn left into Flood Street - Coopers Arms pub (above) on the corner

3

A. At the bottom of Flood Street, take a sharp right along Cheyne Walk before you meet the main road
B. Follow Cheyne Walk along - it curves left at the end up to a junction. Take the pedestrian crossing over to the river side of Chelsea Embankment
C. Cross the Thames over Albert Bridge (above)

4

A. Across the river, turn left into Battersea Park through a pedestrian gate next to a Borough of Wandsworth sign
B. Follow the path as it runs left back towards the river, and head all the way along the waterfront. Halfway along is the Peace Pagoda (above)

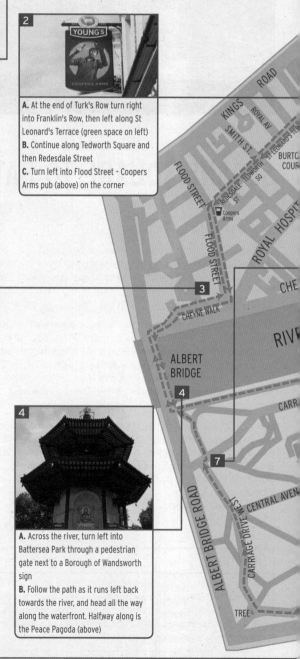

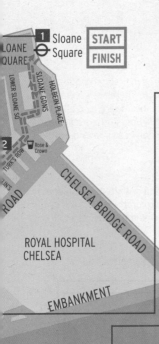

1 Sloane Square

START
FINISH

7

A. Arrive at the Albert Gate (above) – the Carriage Drive turns sharp right
B. Leave the Carriage Drive heading along path that goes forward and left
C. Continue past the Staff Yard and Herb Garden (on right) until the path forks – head left back to the gate you came in
D. Exit the park and retrace your steps back over the river to Sloane Square and the Tube station

ROYAL HOSPITAL CHELSEA

EMBANKMENT

6

A. Follow the path past the running track (on right) - turn left at the end along the road (Carriage Drive East)
B. Continue along the roads past the boating lake (above) on your right on the South Carriage Drive
C. At the end of the South Drive, turn right by the tree set in the road and head along the West Carriage Drive

CHELSEA BRIDGE

5

QUEENSTOWN ROAD

RUNNING TRACK

THAMES

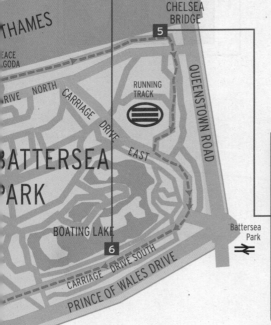

5

A. At the end of the riverfront section, follow the path right uphill (above)
B. Pass in front of the park gates (on left) and take the path that skirts the perimeter of the park
C. Follow the tarmac path as it turns sharp right in front of a wooden fence – ignore the rough trail straight in front

BATTERSEA PARK

BOATING LAKE

6

CARRIAGE DRIVE SOUTH

PRINCE OF WALES DRIVE

Battersea Park

SLOANE SQUARE TO BATTERSEA PARK

Getting there

Start and finish at Sloane Square Tube station (District & Circle Lines - Zone 1).

If you just want to do a loop of Battersea Park, there's an alternative and closer start at Battersea Park overland station (Zone 2).

Opening times

Battersea Park is open from 08.00 through to dusk each day.

Useful links and other info

The Borough of Wandsworth website has useful info on Battersea Park including opening times and access details for the Millennium Arena running track (www.wandsworth.gov.uk).

The Friends of Battersea Park has a website, which includes information on running in the park (www.batterseapark.org/html/running).

Finally, north of the river you're in the Royal Borough of Kensington & Chelsea - their website is www.rbkc.gov.uk.

Signs and maps

Battersea Park has some map boards with 'You Are Here' signs at some of the entrances.

Refreshments

You'll find a couple of street vendors just near the Tube, and a wide variety of shops just down the Kings Road. There is a cafe and other facilities in Battersea Park, but not en route.

Toilets

There is a 20p toilet cubicle machine opposite Sloane Square Tube. There are also toilets in Battersea Park (en route, near the junction of the South and West Carriage Drives).

Parking

The traffic in this area makes getting to and from the start difficult. There are several pricey carparks around Sloane Square, and also limited pay and display parking is available in Battersea Park. We don't recommend driving to this route.

Bike parking

Plenty of bike parking posts outside Sloane Square Tube - they're pretty busy, but it's usually possible to find a free space.

Hills and climbs

Total ascent/descent 13 metres

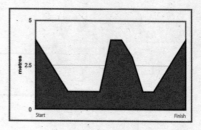

A 4.5 mile virtually traffic-free route along the towpath of the Grand Union Canal from Paddington to the edge of Zone 3

THE GRAND UNION CANAL

Eclectic canalside cruising

Of all the runs in the book this is probably the most traffic free, with only a short section at the end to get you from the canal to the finish at the station. It's then only 15 minutes along the Bakerloo Line back to Paddington.

There are several sections, each with a different feel to them. The start at Paddington is pure Central London with waterside bars and restaurants along the canalside leading to the pleasant Little Venice Basin.

Chic people-watching spots soon give way to a semi-rural feel as you head past Kensal Green Cemetery (explored more fully in route 16). Here the towpath is tree-lined and creates a sense of being well away from the city.

A more industrialised section after Scrubs Lane Bridge serves as a reminder of the canal's working past.

As with all the waterway routes there are some extremely low bridges, which if you're over 6 foot or bounce a lot when you run, can be a bit of a hazard. On this route look out especially for the blue metal bridge just after Little Venice.

Overall, it's a great way to get away from the hustle and bustle.

KEY FACTS

🏃	4.5 miles/7.2 kms
➰	Straight line
🌳	Varied canal towpath
START FINISH	Paddington Tube/mainline station Harlesden Tube/overland station
🕐	Unrestricted
✥	Easy
👟	Hard surfaces throughout LOW BRIDGE HAZARDS
🏃🏃	Very quiet in places
⛰	Pretty flat
🚗	Virtually traffic-free - one road crossing
🚻	Start and just off route
P	Tricky & expensive
🚲	At station
🍽	Near start and en route

THE ROUTE

You start in front of platforms 4, 5 and 6 on the main concourse of Paddington station. Work your way out of the station straight down to the Grand Union Canal. You then follow the towpath for 95% of the route, heading west away from Central London. You pass through Little Venice, and continue on up past Westbourne Green, Kensal Green Cemetery and out past Wilesden. You leave the canal and head up Acton Lane to Harlesden station for the short journey back into town.

THE GRAND UNION CANAL

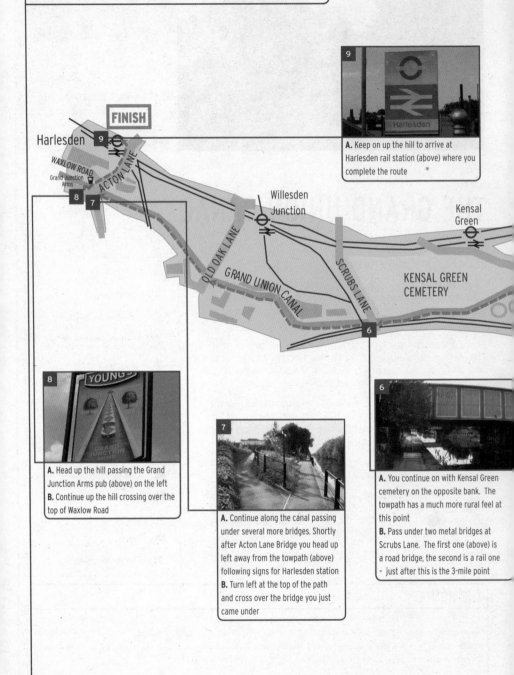

Harlesden

FINISH

WAXLOW ROAD

Grand Junction Arms

ACTON LANE

OLD OAK LANE

GRAND UNION CANAL

SCRUBS LANE

Willesden Junction

Kensal Green

KENSAL GREEN CEMETERY

9 A. Keep on up the hill to arrive at Harlesden rail station (above) where you complete the route

8 A. Head up the hill passing the Grand Junction Arms pub (above) on the left
B. Continue up the hill crossing over the top of Waxlow Road

7 A. Continue along the canal passing under several more bridges. Shortly after Acton Lane Bridge you head up left away from the towpath (above) following signs for Harlesden station
B. Turn left at the top of the path and cross over the bridge you just came under

6 A. You continue on with Kensal Green cemetery on the opposite bank. The towpath has a much more rural feel at this point
B. Pass under two metal bridges at Scrubs Lane. The first one (above) is a road bridge, the second is a rail one – just after this is the 3-mile point

Take care

Be aware of cyclists on the towpath – they don't always slow down for runners. Take care, especially if you've got your MP3 player on. And watch out for those low bridges too.

A. You continue along the towpath, passing under the Westway Flyover again, and further on the Meanwhile Gardens on your left
B. You meet a set of three 'bridges' (first one above) – access points off the canal to small basins. The second of these (next to Sainsbury's supermarket) is the 2-mile point

A. You pass under a metal gated bridge and into Little Venice. Continue along the towpath as it bears around to the left
B. You pass several pleasure boats and cafes. Leave Little Venice behind by passing under a very low blue metal basket-weave bridge
C. You pass the visitor moorings and shortly after a mural made from canal rubbish on the opposite bank (above) at the 1-mile mark

A. You pass along a walkway (above)
B. At the end head left to join the canal towpath
C. Head along the towpath (canal on right). You pass several wine bars and restaurants. Further on you pass under the Westway flyover – look for the Sean Henry sculpture figures on left

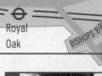

A. In Paddington station make your way to the main arch, so you are standing in front of Platforms 4, 5 and 6 (above)
B. Head to the right past the Heathrow Express Platforms (7 and 8) (signposted for the Hammersmith and City Line Tube platforms)

A. Head along Platform 8 and up the ramp at the end (above)
B. Turn right along a covered walkway (signposted for 'Marks & Spencer & Harrow Road')
C. Turn left at the end of the walkway following sign for 'Little Venice, Sheldon Square, Cannons Health Club'

THE GRAND UNION CANAL

Getting there

The route starts at Paddington station. This is a mainline station and also on the Bakerloo, District, Circle and Hammersmith & City Tube lines. It's in Zone 1.

You need to find your way to the rail concourse in front of platforms 4, 5 and 6 where the route starts.

At the end of the route you're at Harlesden overland/Tube station. The overland service from Watford Junction to Paddington runs along this line. It's also on the Bakerloo line. Most London-bound services go into Paddington in 15 minutes.

Harlesden is in Zone 3.

Opening times

The route isn't affected by specific opening times.

Useful links and other info

The Grand Union canal is looked after by British Waterways. Their website for leisure users is www.waterscape.com/Grand_Union_Canal. If you're planning on doing this route it's worth checking the Waterscape site for towpath closures (under the 'stoppages' section).

Signs and maps

The canal is pretty well signposted. The intermediate rail stations are well flagged from the canal if you want to curtail your run (although once you leave the canal it's not always obvious which way you head to some stations, so take care).

Refreshments

There are all the facilities that you'd associate with a mainline station at Paddington.

At the three 'bridges' at the 2-mile point there is a Sainsbury's supermarket if need to get some groceries on your way.

Toilets

There are toilets at Paddington, and at the aforementioned supermarket half way along.

Parking

Parking is tricky and expensive around Paddington (it'll cost you more than £5 per hour at the station). Consequently we don't recommend driving to this route.

Bike parking

There are bike parking facilities at Paddington.

Hills and climbs

Total ascent 23 metres
Total descent 15 metres

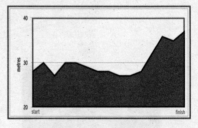

A scenic 4-mile circuit of Hyde Park and Kensington Gardens with the option of adding Green Park and St James's Park for a 6.7 mile loop

HYDE PARK & KENSINGTON GARDENS, GREEN PARK & ST JAMES'S PARK

A classic run through the famous Royal Parks

It's hard to know where to look next when you're running around this part of London. With Buckingham Palace, Kensington Gardens, the Albert and Queen Victoria Memorials, The Serpentine Lake and the Italian Gardens, our route takes in many of the best known landmarks in the city, all set in the fantastic surroundings of some of the most beautiful city parks anywhere in the world.

Sightseeing aside, with four parks all next to each other there are lots of options for tailoring your run to your own requirements, from a 1-mile dash around Green Park to the longer complete circuit that forms our route.

Through Hyde Park and the adjacent Kensington Gardens there's a good mix of top-notch parkland, lakes and ponds, and some real scenic highlights such as the Royal Albert Hall.

Green Park is slightly less noteworthy, but does have the advantage of being a mile loop (using our directions), handy for checking your lap times.

With lakeside running throughout, we think that the route around St James's is the most picturesque of the lot. Enjoy!

KEY FACTS

	4.0 miles/6.4 kms for the main loop (Hyde Park and Kensington Gardens)
	Green Park loop 1 mile/1.6 kms
	St James's loop 1.2 miles/1.9 kms
	The links add on half a mile to make a full circuit 6.7 miles/10.7 kms
	Loop
	Parks, gardens, lakes and ponds with short road sections to link the parks
START FINISH	Hyde Park Corner Tube station
	Restricted
	Fairly easy
	Mixed – tarmac pavements throughout but with grass options in the parks
	Lots of people
	Undulating
	No traffic in the parks, but the links between the parks are across busy roads – use the crossings
	En route
	Tricky & expensive
	None
	Near start and en route

THE ROUTE

From Hyde Park Corner Tube station exit up to street side and head through the Hyde Park Corner doorway. You then head along beside the horse ride and up around the Serpentine Lake. Branch off to head around the Albert Memorial, Round Pond and Italian Gardens, before heading up to the Reformers Tree and then back to Hyde Park corner. Cross over via the Wellington Arch into Green Park and circle around the top of the Park down to the Canada Gates in front of Buckingham Palace. A quick loop of St James's Park Lake and then back through Green Park brings you back to Hyde Park Corner and the Tube station.

HYDE PARK & KENSINGTON GARDENS, GREEN & ST JAMES'S PARKS

5

A. Turn right and immediately take a path back towards the Round Pond
B. Briefly circle the pond clockwise, and then take the second exit path (on the right above), heading towards a tower block in the distance
C. Head all the way along this path, continuing past the Speke Monument up to the Italian Water Gardens

6

A. Head around the Italian Water Gardens keeping them on the right all the time and take the path that runs down the side (above)
B. You arrive at a fork in the path – head down to the right and under the Serpentine Bridge

7

A. After the bridge take the first left. Head up the path and across the road to the car park, then briefly along the path that runs alongside the West Carriage Drive (above)
B. Take a right along a wide shared use path that heads into the park signposted for 'Central Parks Nursery, Rangers Lodge, Storeyard & Old Police House'

[Map of Hyde Park & Kensington Gardens with labels: ROAD, BAYSWATER, ITALIAN GARDEN, SPEKE MONUMENT, WEST CARRIAGE DRIVE, HYDE PARK, REFORMERS TREE, 8, 6, 7, THE BROAD WALK, 5, KENSINGTON GARDENS, ROUND POND, QUEEN VICTORIA STATUE, KENSINGTON PALACE, BANDSTAND, OLD POLICE HOUSE, RANGERS LODGE, SERPENTINE BRIDGE, SERPENTINE GALLERY, CARRIAGE DRIVE, DIANA MEMORIAL FOUNTAIN, THE LIDO, SERPENTINE ROAD, THE SERPENTINE, BANDSTAND, 3, ROTTEN ROW, 2, SOUTH CARRIAGE, KNIG BR, 4, ALBERT MEMORIAL, ALBERT HALL, KENSINGTON ROAD]

4

A. Arrive at the Albert Memorial & Hall (above). Head around the rear of the Memorial and take the path that runs directly away from it into the park (Memorial straight behind you)
B. Head towards, but not all the way up to a mounted statue. Turn left along the shared cycle path (denoted by 'LOOK BOTH WAYS' on the pavement)
C. Head all the way along path (band stand on left) until it meets the Broad Walk path in front of Kensington Palace

3

A. Continue along the path. Follow it as it heads left away from the lake, then past the Lido and Diana Fountain
B. Pass under the Serpentine Bridge and take the first proper path left uphill (slightly back on yourself) towards the road
C. Turn right to take the path that runs parallel to the road (past Serpentine Gallery on right)
D. Continue straight ahead at a junction with a drinking fountain. Pass between two sets of railings around right

2

A. Continue alongside the horse ride ignoring right turns until you come to one which heads up a small incline past a flower bed (above)
B. Turn right and head up to the Serpentine Lake - turn left and head along the path (with the lake on right)

8

A. Head straight on along the path – keep going past the park offices (on right)
B. You arrive at the Reformers Tree site (above) – follow the sign (on the ground) for 'Hyde Park Corner & the Bandstand'
C. Follow the path straight along. At the end head around to the right and over the crossing back to Hyde Park Corner

9

A. To extend the run through Green Park and St James's Park, head over the crossings through the Wellington Arch (above)

GREEN PARK

To add both Green Park and St James's, you split Green Park into two bits doing two sides on the way out and the other bit on the way back from St James's. Or you could just do a loop of Green Park to add the extra mile.

A. From the crossing you arrive at the corner of Green Park with a domed memorial in front of you (above) and the Memorial Gates on the road to your right
B. Head past the dome and take the first path to the left – it runs up alongside the road (on left) and loops around to the right across the top of the park
C. Follow the path all the way around the park to the Green Park Tube station

D. Head past the Tube station and then turn right in front of a wooden food kiosk
E. Follow the path all the way along to arrive in front of the Canada Gate (above) with Buckingham Palace to the right
F. To get to St James's Park, turn left and head around to the pedestrian crossing
G. To get back to Hyde Park corner, turn right and head all the way along the tree line avenue back to the domed memorial to cross over back to the Wellington Arch

---

[Map of Green Park and St James's Park area showing PARK LANE, PICCADILLY, Green Park, QUEEN'S WALK, THE MALL, ST. JAMES'S PARK, HORSE GUARDS ROAD, CONSTITUTION HILL, Hyde Park Corner, BUCKINGHAM PALACE, QUEEN VICTORIA MEMORIAL, BIRDCAGE WALK, St James's Park, START FINISH, with markers 1 and 9]

1

A. Exit the Tube station by the Hyde Park exit. Head through the Hyde Park Corner doorway (above)
B. Take the zebra crossing straight in front and turn left to head along the side of the park. Path runs beside the sandy horse ride (on your left)

ST JAMES'S PARK

Our recommended route is to do a figure of eight loop around the lake using the bridge in the middle (above) twice.
A. From Green Park's Canada Gate, turn left and head around to take the pedestrian crossing over to the corner of St James's Park

B. Bear left down the path (park kiosk on right) into the park and turn left at the lake
C. Head along the lakeside path (lake on right) until you arrive at the bridge
D. Cross over the bridge and turn left to continue circling the lake
E. Arriving at the bridge again, cross over and turn right to complete the loop
F. Take the same pedestrian crossing back over and return to the Canada Gate. Head through Green Park (above) back to Hyde Park Corner and the Tube station

HYDE PARK & KENSINGTON GARDENS, GREEN & ST JAMES'S PARKS

Getting there

The main loop starts and finishes at Hyde Park Corner Park Tube station (Piccadilly Line).

There are plenty of other options – for Green Park use Green Park Tube station (Piccadilly, Victoria Jubilee Lines). Take the exit for Green Park up steps to arrive at point 'Green Park D.' on the route.

For St James's Park you can use St James's Park (District & Circle Lines), and head straight down the road opposite the exit (Queen Anne's Gate) to arrive at the park. The bridge in the middle of the Park is straight ahead along the path from the park entrance.

All stations are in Zone 1.

Opening times

The park opening times vary, but those of Kensington Gardens dictate that the full route can only be done between 06.00 and dusk.

Hyde Park is open from 05.00 to 24.00 each day, Kensington Gardens is open from 06.00 to dusk each day. Green Park is open around the clock. St James's Park is open from 05.00 to 24.00 each day.

Useful links and other info

The Royal Parks website is a fantastic resource for all kind of visitors (www.royalparks.gov.uk), including runners. There are good maps for each of the parks, and listings of events and activities to add to your visit to the parks.

The route passes the Old Police House in Hyde Park, which serves as the offices for the Royal Parks. They're very helpful and can provide you with information leaflets on the parks.

For some of the route you are following the Diana Memorial walk - denoted by the signs set into the path. This is an excellent alternative to our route. A leaflet is available from the park offices.

Signs and maps

There are good information/map boards around the park entrances, with 'You Are Here' pointers.

Refreshments

There isn't a great deal at Hyde Park corner, although there are a couple of street vendors where you can get a drink.

En route there are wooden Royal Parks kiosks (you pass directly by the ones in Green Park and St James's Park) and several proper cafes.

Toilets

There are toilets in the parks. The best en route ones are at the Lido (on the Serpentine Lake in Hyde Park), and near the Italian Gardens in Kensington Gardens.

Parking

Parking is very tricky around Hyde Park Corner and we don't recommend driving to this route. There are car parks near the Serpentine Lake in Hyde Park (pay & display) if you need to bring the car.

Bike parking

There aren't any official bike parking facilities at any of the three Tube stations, and there aren't any obvious places to stash your bike safely. Consequently we don't recommend cycling to this route.

Hills and climbs

Total ascent/descent 37 metres (full circuit)

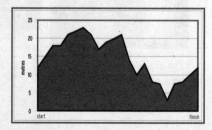

Finding the right run

Lots of people want different things from a run. So we've put together some other listings that will help you find the right run for you

By distance - shortest to longest

Miles/Km	ROUTE	
3.1/5.0	19	Greenwich Circuit
3.2/5.1	25	Regent's Park & Primrose Hill
3.7/5.9	21	The Limehouse Cut
4.0/6.4	13	Thames Loop 1 - Barnes Bridge
4.0/6.4	27	Thames Loop 4 - Westminster & The South Bank
4.1/6.6	7	Southern Explorer - Catford Loop
4.1/6.6	8	Nunhead Cemetery & Peckham Rye
4.2/6.7	6	Hampstead Heath & Highgate
4.2/6.7	20	Hackney Marsh & The River Lee Navigation
4.3/6.9	22	Canary Wharf & The Isle Of Dogs
4.4/7.0	9	Surrey Quays & Rotherhithe
4.4/7.0	28	Sloane Square To Battersea Park
4.5/7.2	26	Thames Loop 3 - Tower Hill & St Paul's
4.5/7.2	29	The Grand Union Canal
4.7/7.5	14	Thames Loop 2 - Putney Bridge
5.0/8.0	4	Northern Explorer - Brent Cross Loop
5.0/8.0	5	Walthamstow Marshes & The River Lee
5.0/8.0	15	Kensal Green & Wormwood Scrubs
5.3/8.5	1	Fryent Country Park & Welsh Harp
5.3/8.5	16	Western Explorer - South Ealing Loop
5.6/9.0	3	Finsbury Park To Ally Pally
5.9/9.4	2	Regent's Canal From Camden Town
6.0/9.6	10	Crystal Palace And Dulwich Village
6.6/10.6	23	London Cemetery & Wanstead Park
6.7/10.7	30	Hyde Park & Kensington Gardens, Green & St James's Park
7.2/11.5	11	Clapham, Tooting & Wandsworth Commons
7.3/11.7	12	Wimbledon Common
7.7/12.3	24	Victoria Park To Limehouse Basin
9.0/14.4	17	Richmond Park Circuit
10.0/16.0	18	Barnes, Kew & Richmond Circuit

By location - principal boroughs

BOROUGH	ROUTE	
BARNET	1	Fryent Country Park & Welsh Harp
	4	Northern Explorer - Brent Cross Loop
BRENT	1	Fryent Country Park & Welsh Harp
	16	Kensal Green & Wormwood Scrubs
BROMLEY	10	Crystal Palace And Dulwich Village
CAMDEN	2	Regent's Canal From Camden Town
	6	Hampstead Heath & Highgate
CITY OF LONDON	26	Thames Loop 3 - Tower Hill & St Paul's
	27	Thames Loop 4 - Westminster & The South Bank
EALING	15	Western Explorer - South Ealing Loop
GREENWICH	19	Greenwich Circuit
HACKNEY	20	Hackney Marsh & The River Lee Navigation
HAMMERSMITH	14	Thames Loop 2 - Putney Bridge
	29	The Grand Union Canal
HARINGEY	3	Finsbury Park To Ally Pally
HOUNSLOW	13	Thames Loop 1 - Barnes Bridge
	15	Western Explorer - South Ealing Loop
ISLINGTON	2	Regent's Canal From Camden Town
KENSINGTON & CHELSEA	28	Sloane Square To Battersea Park
LAMBETH	11	Clapham, Tooting & Wandsworth Commons
LEWISHAM	7	Southern Explorer - Catford Loop
MERTON	12	Wimbledon Common
NEWHAM	21	The Limehouse Cut
REDBRIDGE	23	London Cemetery & Wanstead Park
RICHMOND	13	Thames Loop 1 - Barnes Bridge
	17	Richmond Park Circuit
	18	Barnes, Kew & Richmond Circuit
SOUTHWARK	8	Nunhead Cemetery & Peckham Rye
	9	Surrey Quays & Rotherhithe
	10	Crystal Palace And Dulwich Village
	26	Thames Loop 3 - Tower Hill & St Paul's
TOWER HAMLETS	2	Regent's Canal From Camden Town
	21	The Limehouse Cut
	22	Canary Wharf & The Isle Of Dogs
	24	Victoria Park To Limehouse Basin
WANDSWORTH	11	Clapham, Tooting & Wandsworth Commons
	14	Thames Loop 2 - Putney Bridge
	28	Sloane Square To Battersea Park
WALTHAM FOREST	5	Walthamstow Marshes & The River Lee
WESTMINSTER	25	Regent's Park & Primrose Hill
	27	Thames Loop 4 - Westminster & The South Bank
	29	The Grand Union Canal
	30	Hyde Park & Kensington Gardens, Green & St James's Park

Very hilly climbs (100 metres+)

CLIMB (m)		ROUTE
103	8	Nunhead Cemetery & Peckham Rye
104	12	Wimbledon Common
133	6	Hampstead Heath & Highgate
126	3	Finsbury Park To Ally Pally
142	17	Richmond Park Circuit

Hilly climbs (50 - 100 metres)

CLIMB (m)		ROUTE
53	26	Thames Loop 3 - Tower Hill & St Paul's
73	19	Greenwich Circuit
80	18	Barnes, Kew & Richmond Circuit
82	10	Crystal Palace And Dulwich Village
87	7	Southern Explorer - Catford Loop
88	4	Northern Explorer - Brent Cross Loop
95	1	Fryent Country Park & Welsh Harp

Best views - one from each section

ROUTE		VIEW FROM...
3	Finsbury Park To Ally Pally	...Alexandra Palace over London
7	Southern Explorer - Catford Loop	...Blythe Hill towards Docklands
18	Barnes, Kew & Richmond Circuit	...Richmond Hill back down to the Thames
19	Greenwich Circuit	...the General Woolfe Statue
26	Thames Loop 3 - Tower Hill & St Paul's	....the Millennium Bridge to St Pauls

River and waterside routes

WATERWAY	ROUTE	
RIVER THAMES	9	Surrey Quays & Rotherhithe
	13	Thames Loop 1 - Barnes Bridge
	14	Thames Loop 2 - Putney Bridge
	18	Barnes, Kew & Richmond Circuit
	19	Greenwich Circuit
	22	Canary Wharf & The Isle Of Dogs
	26	Thames Loop 3 - Tower Hill & St Paul's
	27	Thames Loop 4 - Westminster & The South Bank
	28	Sloane Square To Battersea Park
DOLLIS BROOK	4	Northern Explorer - Brent Cross Loop
GRAND UNION CANAL	15	Kensal Green & Wormwood Scrubs
	29	The Grand Union Canal
LIMEHOUSE CUT	21	The Limehouse Cut
REGENT'S CANAL	2	Regent's Canal From Camden Town
	25	Regent's Park & Primrose Hill
RIVER LEE	5	Walthamstow Marshes & The River Lee
	20	Hackney Marsh & The River Lee Navigation
RIVER RAVENSBOURNE	7	Southern Explorer - Catford Loop
RIVER RODING	23	London Cemetery & Wanstead Park

Cemetery routes

CEMETERY	ROUTE	
HIGHGATE	6	Hampstead Heath & Highgate*
KENSAL GREEN	16	Kensal Green & Wormwood Scrubs
	29	The Grand Union Canal*
NUNHEAD	8	Nunhead Cemetery & Peckham Rye
BROCKLEY & LADYWELL	7	Southern Explorer - Catford Loop
CITY OF LONDON	23	London Cemetery & Wanstead Park

*Passed by, not through on these routes

Tube line starts

LINE	ROUTE		LINE	ROUTE	
BAKERLOO	16	Kensal Green & Wormwood Scrubs	VICTORIA	3	Finsbury Park To Ally Pally
	29	The Grand Union Canal		5	Walthamstow Marshes & The River Lee
CIRCLE	25	Regent's Park & Primrose Hill	DISTRICT	12	Wimbledon Common
	29	The Grand Union Canal		14	Thames Loop 2 - Putney Bridge
	26	Thames Loop 3 - Tower Hill & St Paul's		29	The Grand Union Canal
	27	Thames Loop 4 - Westminster & The South Bank		26	Thames Loop 3 - Tower Hill & St Paul's
	28	Sloane Square To Battersea Park		27	Thames Loop 4 - Westminster & The South Bank
				28	Sloane Square To Battersea Park
NORTHERN	4	Northern Explorer - Brent Cross Loop	DLR	19	Greenwich Circuit
	2	Regent's Canal From Camden Town		21	The Limehouse Cut
	11	Clapham, Tooting & Wandsworth		22	Canary Wharf & The Isle Of Dogs
PICCADILLY	3	Finsbury Park To Ally Pally	HAMMERSMITH & CITY	25	Regent's Park & Primrose Hill
	15	Western Explorer - South Ealing Loop		29	The Grand Union Canal
	30	Hyde Park & Kensington Gardens, Green & St James's Park			
CENTRAL	24	Victoria Park To Limehouse Basin	METROPOLITAN	25	Regent's Park & Primrose Hill
EAST LONDON	9	Surrey Quays & Rotherhithe	JUBILEE	22	Canary Wharf & The Isle Of Dogs